God's Daily Word

Jerry Stratton

DEDICATION

To my precious children, Laura Beth and Larry Alan, and their spouses, Michael Nolen and Kimberly Stratton. Laura and Larry have filled my heart with pride and thanksgiving at every stage of their lives. They are wonderful Christian parents to their six beautiful children, our grandchildren. Their prayers and encouragement have been invaluable in the completion of this book.

CONTENTS

ACKNOWLEDGMENTS

I respectfully acknowledge and appreciate the godly business practices and technical expertise of the staff of Armonia Publishing who made the completion of this book possible.

Chuckle: *When his doctor entered the room, the man cried, "My hair is falling out! Can you give me something to keep it in?"*

"Of course," said the doctor reassuringly. He handed the man a small box. "Will this be big enough?"

Quote: *"Put yourself in his place!"* ~ Charles Reade

Treating Others Fairly

"Do not judge, or you too will be judged. For in the same way you judge others, you will be judged, and with the measure you use, it will be measured to you" (Matthew 7:1 NIV).

A favorite pastime for some of us seems to be finding faults in others. We are warned in Scripture to be careful we aren't guilty of the same sins or faults we enjoy pointing out in others. Jesus tells us to remove the plank from our own eye before we become concerned about the speck of sawdust in our brother's eye (see Matthew 7:3 NIV). Here's a story about Charles Reade, the author of our quote for today.

These words, the title of one of Charles Reade's novels, have remained in my memory for more than half a century. The story tells of an English village at a time when workers believed that the introduction of labor-saving machines meant taking bread out of the mouths of their wives and children. Living in this community was Dr. Amboyne. He was a wise physician who tended alike to mill owner and mill worker, to the mind as well as the body. And whenever he found one man denouncing another, he always asked the same question: "What would you do if you were in his place?" ~ Josephus Daniels

It's easy for us to criticize the words or actions of

someone else, and we often do so without understanding the circumstances confronting the person we are criticizing. When we find ourselves denouncing another person we should stop and ask ourselves this question: What would I do if I were in his or her place?

This question then brings us face to face with another important question: What caused this person to act the way he or she did, or what pressures are being brought to bear on that person? We should reserve judgment until we have walked in that person's shoes—until we better understand what the person is going through.

We know that Jesus always dealt with sinful behavior in a loving and redemptive way, never in a condemning way. If we truly care about people and are interested in ministering to them, we will take the time to build relationships and share Christ with them. For wayward Christians, kind, loving, and encouraging words and actions are more effective than harsh criticism and condemnation. Such an approach will help us live out the spirit of the Golden Rule. We will relate to others as we want them to relate to us.

Chuckle: *"My sister has a life-saving tool in her car designed to cut through a seat belt if she gets trapped. She keeps it in the trunk!!!"*

Quote: *"The love we give away is the only love we keep."* ~ Elbert Hubbard

Learning to Think Like Jesus

"Let this mind be in you which was also in Christ Jesus" (Philippians 2:5 KJV).

If we could only learn to think like Jesus and have His attitude, all our problems in living like Jesus would be solved. However, before we can begin to think like Jesus, we must have the desire to do so. Before learning the "how to" must come the "want to."

Prior to Jesus' ascension back into heaven He made some amazing promises. Among them was the promise that He would always be with us in the form of His Holy Spirit. It is His indwelling Spirit that gives us the ability to think like Christ by helping us understand the mind of Christ as revealed in God's Word—to understand how Jesus thinks.

Having said this, what was the mind of Christ really like while He was here on earth? Well, He humbled Himself even unto death and was willing to give up all His own rights as God by coming to earth to save people from their sins, as the Father had planned. He accepted the role of, and had the heart of, a servant. He made Himself nothing so that He could be everything to you and me. He is the supreme example of humility. Likewise, we should be humble servants living our lives for the good of others.

If we allow it, the Spirit of God will teach us to have the mind of Christ. He will teach us to get outside our selfishness and into the lives of others.

One of God's primary purposes for the church is to build bridges of love to the people who need Christ. In John 20:21, Jesus said, *"As the Father has sent me, so I'm sending you."* We must give up the idea that the church is some sort of fortress to protect us from the world and to make us comfortable and cozy with friends who look like us, think like us, talk like us, and act like us. It's true that the church can be a place of comfort and security, but Jesus commissioned the church—Christians—to go where it is uncomfortable.

When we think like Jesus, we will have a love like His for people who are hurting—regardless of their ethnic, economic, or social status. Jesus loved and touched people where they were. *"When he saw the crowds, he had compassion on them, because they were harassed and helpless, like sheep without a shepherd"* (Matthew 9:36 NIV). Jesus was referring to those with desperate physical, emotional, and spiritual needs.

Finally, when we begin to think like Jesus we will adopt His methods in dealing with people. In Luke 6:36, Jesus tells us to *"Be merciful, just as your Father is merciful."* When we think like Jesus we will not say "come to our church," but rather, "we're coming to you."

Rodney Stark was puzzled about how the early Christians, a marginalized and persecuted people, were able to touch so many. In his study he concluded, *"Their sacrifices released an explosion of light the world had never known."*

May 03

Chuckle: *"These days, I spend a lot of time thinking about the hereafter. I go somewhere to get something and then wonder what I'm here after."*

Quote: *"Help me reach a friend in darkness; Help me guide him through the night. Help me show thy path to glory By the Spirit's holy light."* ~ Lorin F. Wheelwright

Dispelling the Darkness

"In him was life; and that life was the light of men. The light shines in the darkness, but the darkness has not understood it. . . The true Light that gives light to every man was coming into the world" (John 1:3b-5, 9 NIV).

The Bible says, *"In the beginning God created the heavens and the earth. The earth was empty, a formless mass cloaked in darkness. And the Spirit of God was hovering over its surface. Then God said, 'Let there be light,' and there was light"* (Genesis 1:1-3 NLT).

Notice how God spoke light into existence—*"Let there be light."* It boggles our minds to think of God doing such things in His creation, but when it came to dispelling darkness with His light, God was just getting started. The next light from God was when He sent His one and only Son, the Light of the World, to dispel the darkness of sin within human souls.

The word "darkness" is used often in God's Word to describe the sinful condition of mankind and the evil of the Prince of Darkness (Satan). The word "light" is used to describe Jesus Christ as He transforms the souls of people into His righteousness and makes us acceptable in God's presence. In John 1:6, we are told that John the Baptist was sent to tell

7

everyone about the "True Light" (Jesus Christ) that was coming into the world—a Light that can never be overcome by darkness.

This means that the darkness of evil never has—and never will—overpower God's light. In the light of Jesus Christ, we see ourselves as we really are—in the darkness of sin and needing a Savior. When we follow Jesus, the True Light, we can avoid walking blindly and falling into sin. He lights the path ahead for us so we can see and know how to live for Him. He removes the darkness from our lives.

Jesus said, *"I am the light of the world. Whoever follows me will never walk in darkness, but will have the light of life"* (John 8:12 NIV). Give your heart and life to Christ, let Him guide your life, and you will never need to stumble in darkness again. He will bring you unspeakable joy, peace, and assurance.

May 04

Chuckle: *Husband: "The bank returned your check."*
Wife: "Good, now I can use it for something else."
Quote: *"This would be a much better world if more*
married couples were as deeply in love as they are in debt."
~ Earl Wilson

Destructive Debt

"Just as the rich rule the poor, so the borrower is servant
to the lender" (Proverbs 22:7 NLT).

The greed of unscrupulous lenders, excessive appetite for possessions by borrowers, and investments in risky mortgage-backed securities by financial institutions brought our country to the depths of recession from which we are now slowly recovering. It's clear that greed and materialism are at the root of our nation's financial problems.

Credit is a good thing when we manage it wisely and do not get in over our heads. By living within our means, we can enjoy the benefits of credit without becoming its slave. However, many are so deeply in debt that they live in a constant state of desperation and anxiety. Indebtedness robs them of the joy of living.

According to 1 Kings 4:29-34, God made Solomon the wisest man on earth. Solomon wrote many of the proverbs in the Bible. He knew that the debtor's life would be dictated by those to whom he owed money, especially if the amount of debt is greater than his ability to pay.

This proverb is not saying we should never borrow. Rather, it implies a warning to examine carefully our ability to pay before entering into a loan arrangement. Such examination should include the possibility of reduced income or even periods of unemployment. We should always take into account unexpected emergencies which could reduce our ability to pay our debts.

A loan handled wisely enables us to do what we couldn't do without it, but a loan which is beyond our ability to handle is disabling and ruinous. Each borrower must realize that until the debt is paid in full, he is the servant of the lending agency or individual from whom the loan was obtained. There's a new golden rule in effect today: *"He who has the gold makes the rules."*

In my ministry, I have counselled with many couples and families whose debt from credit cards, retailers, and mortgage companies was overwhelming, and they could see no way out. Often the indebtedness was putting a strain on marriage relationships and stress within the entire family. I believe that the mishandling of finances is the number-one cause of domestic disharmony and unhappiness.

As Christians, we should incur debt very carefully and we should always pray for God's guidance before entering into any credit agreement. Ask yourself: Will God be pleased with what I'm doing? Is it the right thing to do?

Chuckle: *A police recruit was asked during the exam,
"What would you do if you had to arrest your own mother?"
He answered, "Call for backup."*
Good Thought: *"We need not all agree, but if we disagree,
let us not be disagreeable in our disagreements."*
~ Martin R. DeHaan

Dealing with Disagreements

*"And now I want to plead with those two women, Euodia
and Syntyche. Please, because you belong to the Lord, settle your
disagreement"* (Philippians 4:2 NLT).

Disagreements are inevitable when two or more people
interact. It would be a dull world if we all agreed on everything.
Usually disagreements occur when we don't get our way. Often
we want something done one way and someone else wants it
done another way. Not getting our way can sometimes cause us
to react in anger, frustration, and bitterness to a degree that
others are surprised and taken back by our actions. They may
never have seen this side of us before.

Christians are not immune to immature reactions when
things don't go the way we think they should or the way we
want them to. Sadly, disagreements that lead to anger and
bitterness can destroy the sweet fellowship of God's people.

The two women mentioned in our passage had been co-
workers for Christ in the church at Philippi, and their broken
relationship was a matter of great concern to Paul. Many had
come to know Christ through their cooperative efforts, but the
credibility of their witness was in danger of being destroyed
because they couldn't get along.

We may work hard for Christ's kingdom, but the fruits of our labor can be diminished or non-existent if we can't get along with others in the church. There is no excuse for Christians to be at odds with one another when we are committed to the same cause.

We must remember that when we form strong opinions about something, we are no more entitled to have our opinions accepted by others than others are to have theirs accepted by us. It's a "human" thing to believe that "my idea is the best one and I don't understand why everyone can't see that which is so obvious to me." A Spirit-filled Christian will not allow selfish desires to get in the way of pursuing the common good.

If you find yourself angry and frustrated because you didn't get your way, or things did not go the way you wanted or felt they should, you would be wise to listen more closely to those who disagree with you with the intent to better understand why they feel the way they do. This requires an open mind and a cooperative spirit. We must learn to handle disagreements in a loving and kind way—never with anger and hostility.

"Then make me truly happy by agreeing wholeheartedly with each other, loving one another, and working together with one heart and purpose. Don't be selfish; don't live to make a good impression on others. Be humble, thinking of others as better than yourself" (Philippians 2:2-3 NLT).

May 06

Chuckle: *"We could certainly slow the aging process down if it had to work its way through Congress."* ~ Will Rogers

Quote: *"Life is short, and we have never too much time for gladdening the hearts of those who are traveling the dark journey with us. Oh, be swift to love, make haste to be kind!"* ~ Henri Frederic Amiel

Respect for the Elderly, Part 1

"Never speak harshly to an older man, but appeal to him respectfully as though he were your own father. Talk to younger men as you would to your own brothers. Treat the older women as you would your mother, and treat the younger women with all purity as your own sisters" (1 Timothy 5:1-2 NLT).

In general, there seems to be a growing attitude of disrespect for others in our society. Many have little or no respect for authority and little respect for themselves or others, especially the elderly. I read somewhere that a good measure of a nation's health is the way it treats its elderly. No doubt you have seniors in your family, community, and church who yearn to know they are loved, respected, and appreciated. Their long lives reflect God's honor and blessings on them and have given them the time to increase in knowledge and wisdom. Ignoring this great reservoir of wisdom shows a definite lack of respect on our part.

I don't want to appear self-serving, since I am a member of our older generation, but the seniors in America are deserving of respect and honor because of their tremendous contribution to the building of this great nation. Their perseverance and personal sacrifice have no doubt added significantly to our quality of life, and we owe them much. Many of them are great role models of faithfulness to our Lord and of sacrificial service to others. When you think of all they have done for you, an attitude of love, thanksgiving, and respect should follow.

The Bible is an all-sufficient instructional manual for our inter-personal relationships, both in our biological families as well as our spiritual families. Please note in our 1 Timothy passage that the emphasis is on giving the same respect to all people that you give to your own parents and siblings. The passage assumes respect, honor, and thoughtfulness will be shown to our biological family members and uses this as a model for how we should treat others. Unfortunately, this model of caring and respect is missing in many biological families and sometimes even in spiritual families.

As a pastor, I have made untold numbers of visits to elderly and disabled residents of nursing homes and assisted living centers. It's a joy to see residents regularly receiving expressions of love from family members and friends.

However, I'm saddened when I see mothers, fathers, and grandparents who have been "deposited" in such facilities and seemingly forgotten. Some residents seldom receive visits from family members who show little interest in letting them know they are loved, valued, and respected. This is a terrible tragedy which all of us need to address and do our part to correct.

May 07

Chuckle: *"When you are dissatisfied and would like to go back to youth, think of Algebra."* ~ Will Rogers

Quote: *"When you were born, you cried and the world rejoiced. Live your life in such a way that when you die, the world will cry and you will rejoice."* ~ Unknown Source

Respect for the Elderly, Part 2

"Rise in the presence of the aged, show respect for the elderly and revere your God. I am the LORD" (Leviticus 19:32 NIV). *"Listen to your father, who gave you life, and do not despise your mother when she is old. . . . May your father and mother be glad; may she who gave you birth rejoice"* (Proverbs 23:22, 25 NIV).

In our last lesson we addressed the need to respect and honor all people with emphasis on the elderly. Scriptures are replete with admonitions concerning how we should treat the elderly.

I ran across a Bible lesson by Samuel Simmons on this subject. After a discussion on showing respect to the elderly, he asked the question, "What about you?" Following are his words:

Try to imagine yourself at over 80 years of age. No imagination is required for some of us. Think about how you would want to be treated. When you do, you probably see that patronizing sympathy or superficial pity falls far short of showing respect. What form of respect might you want in your later years? Consider these possibilities:

- The respect that says, "You still matter to God." When you hurt, God cares. When you are lonely,

God is there. When you feel abandoned, God is faithful.

- The respect that says, "You still have purpose in the world."... God invites the elderly to join Him in His kingdom work. When you feel useless, God gives you purpose.
- The respect that says, "I'm interested in your life." What was your vocation? Where did you live? What do you think of this or that national crisis? ... What are the top lessons you have learned in life?
- The respect that says, "God forgives you." Did you make mistakes? Did you hurt others? Do you have regrets? No failure in life lies beyond the powerful forgiveness possible in Jesus Christ.
- The respect that says, "If you need me, I'm here for you." Is someone trying to take advantage of you? Is someone asking you to do something that makes you uncomfortable? Let me know and I will help you if I can.
- The respect that says, "I want to hear your opinion." Do you have a different view than mine? Does your life experience tell you something different? Help me understand what you are thinking. I will listen. *"Is not wisdom found in the aged? Does not long life bring understanding?"*(Job 12:12 NIV).

One final thought from Mr. Simmons: "The way we treat our elders is the model our children and others may use in relating to us when we are old. If that is true, how will those younger persons treat us when we are old? We may be writing the script right now by the way we treat the elderly."

May 08

Chuckle: *"I just had skylights put in my place. The people who live above me are furious!"*

Quote: *"It is by forgiving that one is forgiven."*
~ Mother Teresa of Calcutta

Forgiving Is a Christian Duty

"You must make allowance for each other's faults and forgive the person who offends you. Remember, the Lord forgave you, so you must forgive others. And the most important piece of clothing you must wear is love. Love is what binds us all together in perfect harmony" (Colossians 3:13-14 NLT).

Many of us find it is most difficult to forgive those who have treated us in an unkind or hostile way. Forgiveness is the act of pardoning an offender *in spite* of the offender's shortcomings and errors. It's the last thing Jesus did on the cross! *"Father, forgive them for they do not know what they are doing"* (Luke 23:34 NIV).

When we exercise genuine forgiveness, it frees us from the most powerful bondage we can experience. Jesus didn't say we are to forgive if we feel like it. He said it is a duty, and no limit can be set on the extent of forgiveness. It must be granted without reservations or conditions—by faith and not feelings.

"I'm warning you! If another believer sins, rebuke him; then if he repents, forgive him. Even if he wrongs you seven times a day and each time turns again and asks forgiveness, forgive him" (Luke 17:3-4 NLT).

One of the most effective tools the evil one uses to steal our joy is unforgiveness. With just a little foothold of unforgiveness in our lives, we can easily become bound with chains of bitterness, resentment, anger, and rage. If we let that foothold linger without dealing with it, eventually it will lead to our own self-destruction. But forgiving sets *you* free.

The apostle Paul reminds us that words and emotions can get out of hand—even among Christians. *"But if instead of showing love among yourselves you are always biting and devouring one another, watch out! Beware of destroying one another"* (Galatians 5:15 NLT). When this happens, feelings get hurt, friendships are destroyed, the church becomes divided, and the body of Christ suffers.

It is crucial that each of us asks the Lord daily to help us to *"be kind to each another, tenderhearted, forgiving one another, just as God through Christ has forgiven you"* (Ephesians 4:32 NLT).

A man named John Oglethorpe, in talking with John Wesley, once made the comment, "I never forgive." Mr. Wesley wisely replied, "Then, Sir, I hope that you never sin."
~ Illustrations for Biblical Preaching; Edited by Michael P. Green.

May 09

Chuckle: *When the Duke of Windsor was asked what impressed him most in America, he replied, "the way American parents obey their children."*

Quote: *"When Christians are safe and comfortable, the church is in its greatest danger."* ~ William Arthur Ward

Future Generations

"Future generations will also serve him. Our children will hear about the wonders of the Lord. His righteous acts will be told to those yet unborn. They will hear about everything he has done" (Psalm 22:30-31 NLT).

Whether we're speaking of physical life or spiritual life, healthy societies are highly concerned about the well-being of their future generations. They willingly sacrifice today to make for a better tomorrow for their children and grandchildren. I wonder if our society has lost its way in this area.

We tend to be a self-centered people who want everything to fulfill our own selfish desires, and we want it right now. We see parents who couldn't care less about preparing their children for their future as long as their own selfish appetites are being satisfied today. Socrates said to the people of Athens: *"Why do you turn and scrape every stone to gather wealth and take so little care of your children to whom one day you will relinquish all?"*

I have often heard statements such as: "The church is only one generation away from extinction." Such a statement reflects concern that today's Christians are being negligent in reaching and teaching the next generation of believers. If you and I don't teach our children and grandchildren the things of

God, who will? If not now, when?

In our passage, the Psalmist was confident that God's people would be faithful from generation to generation to proclaim the wonders of God and His righteous. I wonder, is his confidence justified in our time?

The spiritual well-being of yet unborn generations depends upon our faithfulness today. It is God's desire that each generation teach the next, but if we fail to teach our children about the Lord, we risk breaking the chain of God's influence in the generations to come. When we look into the faces of children and teenagers, we see the future leaders in Christianity and our society. Are you and I being faithful in teaching our children and grandchildren the things of God? Are you actively trying to lead them to a saving faith in Jesus Christ?

If we expect our children and grandchildren to grow up serving the Lord, they need to hear about Him from us by our words and the way we live. We should not rely solely on pastors, Sunday School teachers, or others with more knowledge than we to provide their Christian education. They need to hear it from us in the home. *"Teach your children to choose the right path, and when they are older, they will remain upon it"* (Proverbs 22:6 NLT).

How are you and I doing?

May 10

Chuckle: *"Never test the depth of the water with both feet."*

Ponder This: *"Anybody can do their best, but we are helped by the Spirit of God to do better than our best."*
~ Catherine Bramwell-Booth

Finishing the Race

The apostle Paul said of his life, *"I have fought a good fight, I have finished the race, and I have remained faithful"* (2 Timothy 4:7 NLT).

Have you experienced frustration and disappointment from starting a project and not finishing it? I have.

There is a pleasant sense of peace and satisfaction when we complete a task, journey, or assignment—especially when we know we have given it our best effort. I have often asked myself this question: "When I come to the end of my life, will I be able to say with the apostle Paul that I have fought a good fight, I have finished the race, and I have remained faithful to my Lord?"

Paul often used athletic metaphors in describing the Christian life. He pictured Christians competing—not against one another, but for the prize from God awaiting those who faithfully run the race. Paul knew he would be rewarded not by applause of men, but by Christ whom he served. An athlete must begin strong, remain strong, and finish strong if he is to win the race. Some jump out to a quick lead, but begin to fade as they grow fatigued and do not have the reserve strength to finish strong.

Living the Christian life is hard work. It requires

continued effort and commitment, not unlike running a race. You may think that once you receive Jesus Christ as Savior your struggles have ended, but this is not the way Christ works in us. The term "babes in Christ" is used in Scripture to describe new and immature Christians. When we are born again, we are weak baby Christians in the same way a newborn baby is weak and requires a lot of nourishment, exercise, and parental care.

It is God's plan that we grow in strength and knowledge of Him and that we become increasingly more productive for His kingdom. He wants you to grow in your faith and your understanding of His nature and plan for your life. Making a public commitment to Christ is a first step in running the race, but it is only the beginning of a life-long journey of devotion to the cause of Christ.

In ancient Roman athletic games, a laurel wreath was awarded to the winners. As a symbol of triumph and honor, it was the most coveted prize. This is likely what Paul was referring to when he goes on to say, *"And now the prize awaits me—the crown of righteousness that the Lord, the righteous Judge, will give me on that great day of his return. And the prize is not just for me but for all who eagerly look forward to his glorious return"* (2 Timothy 4:8 NLT).

Although Paul would not receive an earthly reward, he would be rewarded in heaven. Whatever you may face—discouragement, hardships, persecution—you can be assured of the reward Christ will give you in eternity. Our faithfulness is proven each day by our tenacious endurance in the race of life.

May 11

Chuckle: *John said to Nathan: "Andrea and I want to get married, but we can't find anywhere to live."*

"Why don't you live with Andrea's parents?" suggested Nathan.

"We can't do that. They're living with their parents."

Quote: *"The believer may well have less use for books on religion than the unbeliever—for how can a man honestly disbelieve unless he has done himself the justice of discovering in what it is he does not believe."* ~ Lionel McColver

What Does "Believe" Mean?

"For God so loved the world that he gave his one and only Son, that whoever believes in him shall not perish but have eternal life" (John 3:16 NIV).

Christians are often called "believers." But what does it mean to believe? Sometimes our modern English language is deficient when translating original biblical languages such as Greek, the primary language of the New Testament. There may not always be an English word that accurately conveys the specific meaning intended by the original writer. Without understanding the broader meanings of a Greek word, we can over-simplify a biblical subject or miss an important truth.

Let's take the word "believe." Today this English word is primarily used to describe our intellectual acceptance of a given proposition or concept as being true. In our passage, the apostle John records the words of Jesus as He tells us we must believe in Him to have eternal life. Sounds simple enough, doesn't it In fact, it sounds so simple that some people may say they believe in Jesus when, in fact, they are only expressing a belief in the facts about Jesus. But our eternal destiny depends on our understanding of the word "believe" as it applies to our relationship with Jesus. How can we know we believe, and how do we explain to an unsaved person what it means to believe?

In our passage, as well as other places in the New Testament, the word "believe" is the translation of the Greek word for "faith" which in its noun form is "pistis" and in its verb form is "pisteuo." In John 3:16, the word translated as "believes" is "pisteuo," which, as amplified by other Scriptures, means to have faith in; to have confidence in; to trust in; to rely upon, to give allegiance to; to commit oneself to. These meanings describe an eternal, growing, and dynamic love relationship with Jesus Christ.

A footnote in the NLT Study Bible: *"To 'believe' is more than intellectual agreement that Jesus is God. It means to put our trust and confidence in him that he alone can save us. It is to put Christ in charge of our present plans (life) and eternal destiny. Believing is both trusting his words as reliable, and relying on him for the power to change."*

To authenticate our own relationship with Jesus Christ, we must understand, accept, and comply with what "believes" really means. When sharing God's plan of salvation, it's imperative that we carefully explain what believing in Jesus entails. We can believe everything the Bible says about Jesus and not believe in Him with a saving faith. Believing about Jesus Christ does not establish a personal relationship with Him.

May 12

Chuckle: *"You know it's going to be a bad day when your birthday cake collapses from the weight of the candles."*

Quote: *"If the devil cannot make you puffed up by pride, he will try to dampen your spirit by discouragement. It's his best tool!"*
~ Unknown Source

Dealing with Discouragement

"Now I am deeply discouraged, but I will remember your kindness" (Psalm 42:6 NLT).

Have circumstances caused you to feel discouraged and ready to throw in the towel and give up? During this recession, you may have lost your job and the search for a new one may have been fruitless. Many of us get discouraged and depressed when things do not turn out the way we had planned or desired. Another translation of our passage says, *"My soul is downcast within me."*

The psalmist was in exile far away from his home in Jerusalem and could not worship his Lord in the Temple. He could not be home for the God-given holidays, when his people remembered all that God had done for them. He was lonely and feeling sorry for himself. He was discouraged.

As a professional soldier for many years, there were times when I was far away from home and family, and I sometimes found myself with a deep sense of discouragement and loneliness—especially when I had to miss special times with my family like anniversaries, birthdays, and Christmas holidays. During those times I needed to turn my attention away from myself and toward God and to focus on His love, mercy, grace, and all that He had done for me. God has always been my anchor and gives me a deep sense of inner peace and contentment.

How does God help you when you are discouraged? He does so in many ways including these:

- He helps by always being with you. *"Never will I leave you;*

never will I forsake you" (Hebrews 13:5b NIV).
- He helps by understanding what you are going through. Jesus said, *"When the world hates you, remember it hated me before it hated you"* (John 15:18 NLT).
- He helps by comforting and strengthening you. *"May our Lord Jesus Christ and God our Father, who loved us and in His special favor gave us everlasting comfort and good hope, comfort your hearts and give you strength in every good thing you do and say"* (2 Thessalonians 2:16-17 NLT).

Notice that the psalmist did not keep his feelings bottled up inside himself. He voiced his feelings to God and fellow worshipers. He was honest in describing his emotional state. I'm reminded of words from an old hymn: *"Take your burdens to the Lord and leave them there."*

If you find yourself discouraged and downcast, take those feelings to your Lord, who will lift you up and carry you through each circumstance. Find someone you love and trust with whom to share your burdens and be encouraged.

May 13

Chuckle: *"Adolescence is that period when a boy refuses to believe that someday he will be as ignorant as his parents."*

Quote: *"He who believes is strong; he who doubts is weak. Strong convictions precede great actions."* ~ J. F. Clarke

Disowning Our Lord

Jesus said to Simon Peter, *"I tell you the truth, . . . this very night, before the rooster crows, you will disown me three times." But Peter declared, "Even if I have to die with you, I will never disown you." And all the other disciples said the same"* (Matthew 26:34-35 NIV).

Jesus had predicted His death and resurrection to His disciples. On the night before He was crucified, Jesus ate the Passover meal with them. There He identified Judas Iscariot as the one who would betray Him into the hands of His enemies. Jesus went on to tell His disciples that they would all lose courage and "fall away" from Him.

Sure enough, when Jesus was arrested, all the disciples deserted Him and fled, even though they had all said they never would—even if it meant their deaths.

However, Peter followed at a distance as they took Jesus away. After Jesus was taken before the high priest and the whole Sanhedrin, Peter was confronted three times by people who accused him of being a follower of Jesus. Each time Peter vehemently denied that he even knew Jesus. After he had denied/disowned Jesus the third time, the rooster crowed.

"Then Peter remembered the word Jesus had spoken: 'Before the rooster crows, you will disown me three times.' And he went outside and wept bitterly" (Matthew 26:75 NIV).

As Christians most of us—if asked—would say as the disciples did: "I will never disown my Lord." But how bold are we in being identified with Him? How bold are we in expressing our faith before others out of fear of what they might say or do? How bold are we in letting others know of our allegiance to Christ in the workplace, classroom, or family gatherings?

We may be disowning our Lord by our actions—by the way we live and our silence about our relationship with Him. How much evidence is there in your life and mine that we are fully devoted followers of Christ? Is your love for your Lord overshadowed by a fear of what others may think or say about you?

Like Peter, a time will come when we will deeply regret our failure to be identified with the One who loved us so much that He died for us.

May 14

Chuckle: *"A real Christian is a person who can give his pet parrot to a town gossip."* ~ Billy Graham

Quote: *"The Christian is one who has forever given up the hope of being able to think of himself as a good man."* ~ Leslie Newbigin

Everyone Who Believes

"We are made right in God's sight when we trust (have faith) in Jesus Christ to take away our sins. And we all can be saved in this same way, no matter who we are or what we have done" (Romans 3:22 NLT).

Here Paul gives a beautiful paraphrase of John 3:16, where Jesus said, *"For God so loved the world that he gave his only Son, so that <u>everyone who believes</u> (trusts, has faith) in him will not perish but have eternal life."*

Genuine Christians are those who have acknowledged that Jesus Christ, as the Son of God, has paid the penalty for their sins on the cross. They have repented of their sins and their souls have been saved from eternal punishment by God's grace through their faith in Jesus Christ as Savior and Lord. They have made a conscious decision to entrust their lives into Christ's care and have accepted His forgiveness of their sins, granting Him complete Lordship over their lives. Jesus called this being "born again." A summary definition of a Christian is: one in whom Jesus dwells; one whose life Jesus controls; and one through whom Jesus is revealed.

I have heard many different answers to the question: Are you a Christian? One response is 'I'm a Christian because someone close to me is a Christian'—for example, 'my father was a deacon.' Or 'my parents raised me in a Christian home.'

I call this an attempt at "vicarious" Christianity. Although one is more likely to be saved and become a Christian if reared in a Christian environment, living in a Christian home does not make you a Christian any more than standing in a garage makes you a car.

Becoming a Christian requires a transformation of a person by the power of the Holy Spirit. *"What this means is that those who become Christians become new persons. They are not the same anymore, for the old life is gone, A new life has begun"* (2 Corinthians 5:17 NLT). *"And as the Spirit of the Lord works within us, we become more and more like him, Christ, and reflect his glory even more"* (2 Corinthians 3:18 NLT).

Others think they are right with God if they do their best to live a good moral life and maybe even attend church services now and then. In other words, they think we are saved by what we do rather than by what Jesus did on our behalf. We live in a world where we work for what we receive and it's difficult for some to understand that we don't have to work for our salvation—it is a gift from God.

However, we do good works in obedience to God because we have been saved, not in order to be saved. *"For we are God's masterpiece. He has created us anew in Christ, so that we can do the good things he planned for us long ago"* (Ephesians 2:10 NLT).

If living a "good" life could save us, why did Jesus need to die?

May 15

Chuckle: *A preacher up in the Adirondacks went to church one Sunday morning. The pastor called on him to pray. He replied—"Pray yourself, I'm on vacation!"*

Quote: *"As a moth gnaws a garment, so doth envy consume a man."* ~ Chrysostom

Envy Destroys

"Do not covet your neighbor's house. Do not covet your neighbor's wife, male or female servant, ox or donkey, or anything else your neighbor owns" (Exodus 20:17 NLT).

Coveting is a strong desire to have the possessions of someone else. Such desire goes far beyond merely admiring a person's possessions, or thinking "I really would like to have one of those." When you covet you can easily progress to the point of resenting the person who has what you don't. This is envy. When we envy, we transfer our feelings of desire for a person's possessions to resentment against the person.

You may be envious of someone for what he or she has, or the praise he or she has received, or the success he or she has attained. God saw that such feelings could arise in the hearts of His people. He knew that coveting is such a destructive force that He chose to deal with it in the Ten Commandments. God knows possessions alone can never bring lasting happiness. He also knows that greed, jealousy, covetousness, and envy can destroy relationships among His people, and between His people and Himself.

Not only can such desires take away our joy, they can lead us to commit other sins such as adultery and stealing—both of which are also forbidden in the Ten Commandments. In our society, we often see violence committed against someone by another who is driven by envy. But envy can easily create bitterness and destroy relationships among believers as well. Being covetous and envious is a counter-productive exercise since God is able to provide what we really need, even if He chooses to stop short of giving us everything we want. To avoid being envious, we need to practice being content with what we have.

"Not that I was ever in need, for I have learned how to get along happily whether I have much or little. I know how to live on almost nothing or with everything. I have learned the secret of living in every situation, whether it is with a full stomach or empty, with plenty or little" (Philippians 4:11-12 NLT). Once Satan gains a foothold in your life by creating envy in your heart, he can destroy the joy and peace that God wants you to have.

There is a fable that Satan's agents were failing in their various attempts to draw into sin a holy man who lived as a hermit in the desert of northern Africa. Every attempt had met with failure, so Satan, angered with the incompetence of his subordinates, became personally involved in the case.

He said, "The reason you have failed is that your methods are too crude for one such as this. Watch this." He then approached the holy man with great care and whispered softly in his ear, "Your brother has just been made Bishop of Alexandria." Instantly the holy man's face showed that Satan had been successful—a great scowl formed over his mouth and his eyes tightened up.

"Envy," said Satan, "is often our best weapon against those who seek holiness."

May 16

Chuckle: *Beautician: Did that mud-pack I gave you for your girlfriend improve her appearance?*

Man: It did for a while—but then it fell off.

Quote: *"Ninety-nine percent of the failures come from people who have the habit of making excuses."* ~ Dr. George Washington Carver

Excuses

Jesus replied, *"A certain man was preparing a great banquet and invited many guests . . . But they all alike began to make excuses"* (Luke 14:16, 18 NIV).

In our passage, Jesus was teaching His followers through a parable about a great banquet that God is preparing, and He is inviting all of us to the celebration. But many who were invited began to make excuses for not accepting the invitation.

You may have heard the saying: "If you don't want to do something, one excuse is as good as another." This begs the question: Why are so many of God's people too busy to do His bidding?

I have often heard this excuse, and regretfully, I've used it myself—"I just have too much on my plate right now" to serve God more fully and faithfully. We can all be certain it isn't God who has filled our plates. We do that ourselves with all the things that take our time, energy, and other resources. Often, our plates are filled with everything except the most important— God's plan for our lives.

In Jesus' story, many people turned down the banquet invitation because the timing was inconvenient. They had other more pressing demands on their time. We too may resist or postpone our response to God's invitation, and the excuses we offer may sound perfectly reasonable. You may use work requirements, family responsibilities, financial needs, etc. But make no mistake, God's invitation—whether it be for salvation or for Christian service—is the most important bidding in our lives, no matter how inconvenient the timing may seem.

As a Christian, if you find yourself making excuses for not making time for answering God's call to service, please remember the Holy Spirit who dwells within you. If you will allow Him to help you filter out all the "junk" that's on your plate, you will suddenly realize that you have time for God, family, work, etc.

If the Holy Spirit has convicted you in this area, let Him help you readjust your priorities. What are you willing to give up to accept God's invitation? Just give God complete control of your life and your problem will be solved.

If you have never received Christ as Savior, please respond to His invitation by placing your trust in Him today. You have no guarantee of tomorrow. Without making excuses, just ask Him to forgive your sins and come into your heart and life as Savior and Lord.

May 17

Chuckle: *A little girl was diligently pounding away on her grandfather's word processor. She told him she was writing a story. "What's it about?" he asked.*

"I don't know," she replied. "I can't read."

Quote: *"One of the mysteries of faith is that, although it constitutes our deepest response to God for what he has done for us in Jesus Christ, yet it is, at the same time, a gift from him when we lift our eyes beyond ourselves. He meets us with faith when we want to have faith."* ~ John Gunstone

Faith Produces True Peace

"Your faith has made you well; go in peace" (Luke 8:48 NASB). *"Peace I leave with you; my peace I give you"* (John 14:27 NIV).

Can you imagine how the woman in this passage must have felt (see Luke 8:43-48)? She had been sick for over twelve years and had found no person or treatment that could offer relief from her infirmity. She was desperate, and when she learned that Jesus was near she was determined to see Him and at least touch Him in hopes that He would heal her. In fact, it seems her faith was so strong that she knew—without doubt—that touching such a man of God would heal her.

Picture the great throng of people around Jesus. It must have been a physically exhausting effort for a woman who was not well just to plow through the crowd and get close enough to touch Him. The result of her faith was that Jesus' healing power was released into her the instant she touched His garment, and she was healed. What a beautiful picture of God's power and amazing love for each of us, regardless of what we may be going through in life.

Please notice that physical healing occurred, but perhaps an even greater gift was granted to the woman—a peace that only God can give. As we hold onto God in faith, He may or may not choose to heal us physically, but He certainly will grant us strength, comfort, and <u>peace</u> to deal with whatever may be troubling us. *"And the peace of God, which transcends all understanding, will guard your hearts and minds in Christ Jesus"* (Philippians 4:7 NIV).

It was the woman's faith that released Christ's power into her life. Are you casually aware of who Jesus is or do you actively reach out to Him in faith knowing He can bring miraculous physical healing as well as spiritual healing?

Renew your faith today and reach out to Jesus the Savior of our souls, the Great Physician, and giver of peace —His peace.

May 18

Chuckle: *Diner: "Waiter! You have your finger on my steak!"*
Waiter: "Well, I don't want it to fall on the floor again."
Quote: *"God the Father of our Lord Jesus Christ increase us in faith and truth and gentleness, and grant us part and lot among His Saints."*
~ St Polycarp

Fear or Faith

"God is able to do superabundantly, far over and above, all that we dare ask or think. Infinitely beyond our highest prayers, desires, thoughts, hopes, or dreams" (Ephesians 3:20 AMP). *"According to your faith, it will be done to you"* (Matthew 9:29 NIV).

We can approach life in one of two ways—by fear or by faith. If we live by fear, we will view every circumstance with pessimism and concentrate on what we're afraid will happen, rather than what we want and expect to happen. Even Job, the great man of faith, found himself living by fear. *"What I feared has come upon me; what I dreaded has happened to me"* (Job 3:25 NIV).

Or you can live by faith and view every circumstance with optimism. If we live by faith, we expect God's promised presence and power to be available to us in every situation and will not allow ourselves to live with fear and dread.

Unfortunately, many Christians never tap into God's abundant resources made available to us by God Himself. We know, intellectually, that God is all powerful and can distribute that power whenever and wherever He chooses.

However, because of our lack of faith, we miss seeing the evidence of God's power. There have been times in my life when I prayed but didn't really expect God to do what I asked. My expectations translated into a lack of faith. The key that unlocks God's power in your life is really simple. It's faith. The law of expectations says we get what we expect in life. We see what we expect to see, feel what we expect to feel, act the way we expect to act, and eventually, achieve what we expect to achieve.

Your expectations influence your happiness, your relationships, and even your health. Because of our faith, or lack of faith, our expectations as to what God will do influence what God actually does. This is because *"according to your faith, it will be done to you."*

The words of Jesus, in our text, tell us Jesus did not immediately respond to the pleas of some blind men to have their sight restored. Jesus waited to see if they had faith. There may have been times in your life when you thought God wouldn't answer your prayers, or was much too slow in answering. It could be that God was testing your faith as Jesus did with the blind men. Do you desire and expect God's help in dealing with your problems?

Fear and faith are demonstrated in the story of David and Goliath. In fear, everyone but David saw the giant as too big and powerful for them to defeat. But by faith, David saw him as a target much too big for him to miss with his deadly slingshot.

What are your Goliaths in life and how do you approach them—by fear or by faith?

May 19

Chuckle: *"The Japanese eat very little fat and suffer fewer heart attacks than the British or Americans. On the other hand, the French eat a lot of fat and also suffer fewer heart attacks than the British or Americans. Conclusion: Eat what you like. It's speaking English that's killing you!"*

Quote: *"Close your eyes to the faults of others, and you open the doors of friendship."* ~ William Arthur Ward

Finding Faults in Others

Jesus said, *"Why do you look at the speck of sawdust in your brothers eye and pay no attention to the plank in your own eye? How can you say to your brother, 'Let me take the speck out of your eye,' when all the time there is a plank in your own eye?"* (Matthew 7:3-4 NIV).

If we aren't careful we will catch ourselves feeling some sort of perverse pleasure from pointing out faults in others, while at the same time having difficulty seeing our own. Sometimes a startling realization comes over us when we discover that the faults in others that are so bothersome to us are the very traits we find in ourselves. Often our own bad habits and weaknesses are the very ones we most want to point out in others.

We can find it much easier to magnify the faults of others while finding excuses or justifications for our own. Perhaps this is because we experience satisfaction by classifying our own faults as serious only when seen in others. By seeing ourselves in the shadow of someone else's faults, we can feel better and not be so concerned about the relative insignificance of what we see to be our own.

Jesus tells us to examine our own motives and actions rather than sitting in judgment of others. Jesus said this in verses 1-2 of our chapter: *"Stop judging others, and you will not be judged. For others will treat you as you treat them. Whatever measure you use in judging others, it will be used to measure how you are judged."*

Jesus is identifying the kind of hypocritical attitude that wants to tear down someone else in order to make oneself be seen in a more favorable light—trying to make ourselves look better at the expense of others.

We are wise if we look at ourselves in the mirror of God's Word before focusing our attention on the faults of others. After doing this, you may be surprised at how your desire to find faults in others will diminish. You will likely become increasingly concerned with asking God's help and forgiveness in dealing with your own faults.

A man was applying for the job of private secretary to Winston Churchill. Before introducing him, an aunt of Churchill's told the man, "Remember, you will see all of Winston's faults in the first five hours. It will take you a lifetime to discover all his virtues."

May 20

Chuckle: *"What kind of man was Boaz before he married? Ruthless!"*

Quote: *"I think that God means that we shall do more than we have yet done in furtherance of his plans and he will open the way for our doing it."* ~ Abraham Lincoln

God Has Plans for You

"The Lord will work out <u>his plans</u> for my life—for your faithful love, O Lord endures forever" (Psalm 138:8 NLT).

Everyone dreams and makes plans for the future. I enjoyed a recent TV commercial that showed several retirement age people saying, "when I grow up, I want to . . . " Each one filled in the blank with his or her dream.

Those who do not know Christ as Savior and Lord have only their own wisdom and skills to bring their dreams and plans to fruition. But to experience what is best for you in life, you must make your plans and dreams compatible with God's plans.

If you believe that God has a plan for your life, you may be wondering what that plan really is. He alone knows what is best for us, and He alone can lead us to fulfill His plan for each of us.

Your ultimate purpose is to please God. You and I were created for God's pleasure, and God's plan is for each of us to fulfill His purpose. You may not fully understand what God is doing in your life, where He is leading you, or what He wants to accomplish through you. But the most important question is this: Do you trust God and believe that He knows where He wants you to go and the person He wants you to become?

Whether or not you fully understand God's plan for your life, your faith should include a firm belief in God and that He wants you to fulfill His purpose for your life. Furthermore, each of us should trust Him to lead us and bring us to our final destination. *", . . . But the Lord's plans stand firm forever; his intentions can never be shaken"*

(Psalm 33:11 NLT). God is completely trustworthy—His intentions never change.

Regardless of your age or circumstances, God has plans for your life, and God's plans are what matters—not yours. Knowing and doing what God has planned for us should be our first priority. If so, we will trust Him completely to lead us in a way that will bring them to complete fulfillment.

"Many, O Lord my God, are the wonders you have done. The things you planned for us no one can recount to you; . . . they would be too many to declare" (Psalm 40:5 NIV).

"We can make our plans, but the Lord determines our steps. Commit your work to the Lord, and your plans will succeed" (Proverbs 16:9, 3-4 NLT).

May 21

Chuckle: *"This lady said she recognized me from the vegetarian club, but I'd never met herbivore."*

Quote: *"Righteousness is one thing, self-righteousness is another. May God keep me from ever confusing them."* ~ Lionel Blue

Brand New Nature

"Put on your new nature, and be renewed as you learn to know your Creator and become like him" (Colossians 3:10 NLT).

Most of us don't have much difficulty with our conduct while we have our church face on, along with our Sunday clothes. It's those other six pesky days that give us the most trouble.

When Paul says we are to be clothed with a new nature, he means that our conduct every day should match our professed faith. If we say we are Christians, we should act like it. Our conduct should always reflect our new nature. But if you are like I am, my actions don't always measure up, in spite of my best intentions. My spiritual clothing sometimes becomes soiled and tattered.

Putting on the new nature is a straightforward action that is as simple as putting on clothing. However, Paul recognized that our new nature requires renewing every day we live. In the same way that we change into clean and fresh clothing each day, our new nature must be cleaned and made fresh as we continually learn more about Christ with the intent to be like Him.

God's answer to our failures is to extend us the privilege of a brand new start each morning—to avail ourselves of Christ's Spirit living within us and allow Him to teach us. Christians should be in a continual, never ending spiritual education program. The more we learn about Christ and His work, the more like Him we become. Christ-like humility will become more and more natural to us. *"Your attitude should be the same as that of Christ Jesus"* (Philippians 2:5 NIV).

Becoming like Christ is a life-long process and we will never be perfect as Christ is perfect. However, like Paul, we can say, *"I don't mean to say that I have already achieved these things or that I have already reached perfection! But I keep on working toward that day when I will finally be all that Christ Jesus saved me for and wants me to be"* (Philippians 3:12 NLT).

A brand new life every day really is possible if we determine to *"grow in the grace and knowledge of our Lord and Savior Jesus Christ. To him be glory both now and forever! Amen"* (2 Peter 3:18 NIV).

May 22

Chuckle: *When God finished the creation of Adam, He stepped back, scratched His head, and said, "I can do better than that!"*

Quote: *"Who is the third who walks always beside you? When I count, there are only you and I together. But when I look ahead up the white road There is always another one walking with you."* ~ T. S. Eliot

By God's Spirit

"Not by might nor by power, but by my Spirit," says the Lord Almighty" (Zechariah 4:6 NIV). *"But as for me, I am filled with power, with the Spirit of the Lord"* (Micah 3:8a NIV).

Do you ever feel overwhelmed by the challenges you face with each day? You may feel that the problems facing you are just too great to overcome. Do they seem too massive for you to handle? When you awake, do you say "good morning Lord," or "Good Lord, it's morning?" Did you feel this way when you awoke this morning and thought about the day ahead?

We must remember that we serve an all-knowing God. He knows about and understands everything that concerns you and fully recognizes your inability to handle life's challenges in your own strength. But He enables you to face them in the power of His Spirit. This means we are not limited by our own abilities and wisdom, but have the unlimited resources of our heavenly Father at our disposal if we but trust and rely on Him in every situation.

Many believe that to survive and excel in this life they must be tough, self-reliant, strong, independent, and unwavering. But God tells us that in our weakness, the strength of His Spirit is revealed. It's only in the power of the Spirit that anything gets done that has lasting value. Jesus said, *"apart from me you can do nothing"* (John 15:5c NIV).

It's easy for us to say we trust God's Spirit to guide and teach us. But at the same time, we go through life trying to solve our problems in our own strength as if He doesn't exist.

I'm reminded of the funny story about a man who was working on the steep roof of his house. He lost his footing and was tumbling toward the eave and the inevitable life-threatening fall to the ground. In his plight he prayed, "Lord, please save me!" Then with relief in his voice he said, "Oh, never mind Lord; I've caught on a nail." This humorous little story reminds us that if he had truly been depending upon God's Spirit, he would have prayed something like this: "Thank you, Lord, for placing that nail where it would break my fall." How many times do we fail to give credit to God for inexplicable occurrences that we call good luck or good fortune, or credit them to our exceptional abilities.

Today, let's pledge together to live for God with complete trust in Him rather than our own strength. Let's seek Him in every situation and we will be amazed at what God can accomplish in us and through us in the power of His Spirit.

May 23

Chuckle: *The sign on a church nursery door read: "We will not all sleep, but we will all be changed." (See 1 Corinthians 15:51)*
Quote: *"Blessed are they who have nothing to say and who cannot be persuaded to say it."* ~ James Russell Lowell

Consideration for Others

"You say, 'I am allowed to do anything'—but not everything is helpful. You say, 'I am allowed to do anything'—but not everything is beneficial. Don't think only of your own good. Think of other Christians and what is best for them" (1 Corinthians 10:23-24 NLT).

An underlying principle that runs throughout the entire Bible is that of loving and doing good for one's neighbors—other people. Along with this principle comes the realization that when we focus on bringing good to others, we are bringing good to ourselves.

Within this passage is one of the most difficult lessons we need to learn as believers. How well we learn it depends upon our own level of spiritual maturity. As we mature, the Holy Spirit will teach us that a word or an action that isn't necessarily wrong can still cause a weaker believer to become confused, disillusioned, and hurt. For example, telling a truth about someone in an inconsiderate and unkind way can do terrible damage to the spiritual moral and confidence of that person.

Here Paul gives us a simple rule of thumb to help us make decisions about our actions. We should always be sensitive and gracious to others. While we have great freedom in Christ, as opposed to the Old Testament law, we should never use that freedom at the cost of hurting a Christian brother or sister. The welfare of others should be more important to us than our own.

We live in a "what's in it for me" society where the focus is selfishly placed on me, myself, and I. Society encourages people to seek everything for their own benefit, and when they do, they are praised and admired for it. Obviously, this lesson does not mean we should not look out for our own best interests, but it is teaching us to place priority of our actions on bringing good to others. In 1 Corinthians 8:13, Paul tells us that he would never do anything that would cause another weaker Christian to stumble.

When I was a child growing up in a small rural community, I loved to go to the movies on Saturday afternoons. But some Christians viewed the movie theater as a "den of iniquity." One Saturday I asked my pastor father to go with me to see a movie. I think it was "Black Beauty," or something like that. I'll never forget my father's answer. He said, "Son, it would not be wrong for me to go and I would like to go with you. But if I did, it would offend those who believe otherwise. It would diminish my influence and reputation as a pastor in their eyes and perhaps cause them to stumble in their faith. Therefore, I cannot go."

His sensitivity to the feelings of others, not what he could do or wanted to do, dictated his actions.

May 24

Chuckle: *"The Pillsbury Doughboy died yesterday of a yeast infection and complications from repeated pokes in the belly. He was 74."*

Quote: *"All deception in the course of life is indeed nothing else but a lie reduced to practice, and falsehood passing from words into things."* ~ Robert South

The Art of Deception

"See to it that no one takes you captive through hollow and deceptive philosophy, which depends on human tradition and the basic principles (evil powers) of this world rather than on Christ" (Colossians 2:8 NIV).

Make no mistake—the father of all deception is Satan himself. To deceive is to "make someone believe what is not true; fool or trick; mislead; or defraud." We all need to understand that deception is the opposite of that which is true.

There is so much deception in our society today that it is becoming increasingly difficult to distinguish real from fake, true from false, trustworthy from unreliable. Many political ads are classic deceptions as half-truths, innuendos, distortions, and outright lies. They are used to deceive the public about political opponents.

Those most susceptible to spiritual deception are those not well founded in the truths in God's Word. If we know what we believe and why we believe it, we are much less likely to be deceived.

Is your Christian faith based on the fact that you were raised by Christian parents or is it based on your own study of the Bible and your personal commitment of your life to Jesus Christ? If you don't have a firm basis for your faith, you can become prey for the occult and false religions of all kinds. We see all sorts of "religious sects" with just enough truth in their teachings to appear genuine.

Young people who are trying to find answers to life's questions are particularly susceptible to being deceived. Many are intrigued by the "far out" and bizarre. Many cults use clever seduction techniques for luring young people into strange and mystical rituals. Also, many young people have little or no foundation of truth with which to compare what they are reading and hearing. It's important for parents to teach their children the truths of God's Word to help them defend against being deceived.

False teachers can also be found in the church, as Paul witnessed in the church at Corinth. *"False apostles, deceitful workers transform themselves into apostles of Christ"* (2 Corinthians 11:13 NKJV). Scripture predicts this kind of apostasy will continue to grow until Christ returns.

How can we prepare ourselves and our children to avoid being deceived spiritually, politically, or morally?

- Be a serious student of God's Word.
- Know what you believe and why you believe it.
- Practice your faith by keeping your own life pure and uncompromising.
- Become knowledgeable of the political issues as you prepare to vote when elections are held.
- Study the records and listen carefully to the words of the candidates.

May 25

Chuckle: *"Middle age is when you choose your cereal for the fiber, not the toy."*

Quote: *"Praise, my soul, the King of heaven, To His feet thy tribute bring."* ~ Henry Frances Lyte

The Endorsement That Matters

"This is my Son, whom I love; with him I am well pleased. Listen to him!" (Matthew 17:5 NIV).

Endorsements are important to us in many ways. When politicians are running for office, they value the endorsements of large newspapers, other prominent groups, and influential leaders. It adds credibility to their candidacies when a long list of endorsements have been given them.

Likewise, when a person is looking for a job, it helps if letters of recommendation accompany his or her resume. We depend on the opinions of others to help us gain the respect, approval, and support we desire.

When Jesus was ministering here on earth, His identity was a major topic of conversation. Not everyone accepted His credentials as the promised Messiah. On the contrary, many not only did not believe He was who He said He was, but some even accused Him of blasphemy and being a representative of Satan.

Jesus' closest disciples had accepted Him as the Son of God and wanted others to believe as well. When Christ was transfigured before Peter, James, and John, He was seen conversing with two giants of faith, Moses and Elijah (see Matthew 17:1-13). In the minds of the disciples, this experience served as a powerful convincing endorsement of Jesus and solidified their confidence in His identity. As a result, it's no surprise that they wanted to tell everyone about it.

But in our passage, the only endorsement that really mattered to Jesus was the one from God, His Father. This should be true in our own lives. As Christians, our service should be to please

God, not other people. Of course, it makes us feel good when fellow Christians give us their endorsement with kind words of praise and encouragement. But the receipt of such accolades should not be our motivation for service. Like Jesus, we should only be concerned about doing the will of the Father, even if the praise of other people does not come.

Perhaps these words from Paul will put endorsements in the proper perspective: *"Obviously, I'm not trying to be a people pleaser! No, I am trying to please God. If I were still trying to please people, I would not be Christ's servant"* (Galatians 1:10 NLT).

Each of us should ask, "Who am I trying to please when I render service to others?" Let's commit ourselves to seeking the approval of our Lord in all we do because His approval—endorsement—is the only one that really matters.

May 26

Chuckle: *Children were in the cafeteria line of a Christian elementary school. The first item was a stack of apples. A teacher had placed a note on the apples, "Take only one, God is watching."*

At the end of the line was a large stack of chocolate chip cookies. In childish writing was a note. "Take all you want—God is watching the apples!"

Quote: *"Without faith a prayer has only form. Without faith a prayer has not heart or flame."* ~ Guy Everton Tremaine

Faith and Prayer Power

"Whatever you ask for in prayer, believe (have faith) that you have received it and it will be yours" (Mark 11:24 NIV).

How can I pray with faith and power? The first truth we must understand is that it is only in the name of Jesus that we can come to the Father in prayer. Jesus said: *"I am the way and the truth and the life. No one comes to the Father except through me"* (John 14:6 NIV).

Not only must we come to the Father through faith in Jesus Christ for salvation, we must also come to the Father in prayer in the name of Jesus. Thus, we close our prayers with words like: "I pray/ask these things in the name of Jesus. Amen."

Jesus told His disciples that they could ask for anything in His name and it would be given them. *"And I will do whatever you ask in my name, so that the Son may bring glory to the Father"* (John 14:13 NIV). This sounds as if we can ask anything our little thumping hearts desire and Jesus is obligated to give it to us. Is this true?

Listen to the conditions Jesus describes for this kind of praying. *"If you remain in me and my words remain in you, ask whatever you wish, and it will be given to you"* (John 15:7 NIV).

What does it mean to "remain in Jesus?" It means that we stay connected to Him through faith, study of His Word, prayer, and yielding control of our lives to His Holy Spirit who *"lives with you and is in you"* (John 14:17 NIV). Jesus used the analogy of a vine and its branches to help us visualize this "remaining" in Him. *"I am the vine; you are the branches . . . apart from me you can do nothing"* (John 15:5 NIV).

Think with me about the relationship of a tree trunk to its branches. All the life-sustaining nutrients, genetic instructions to bear fruit, and life-giving moisture come to the branches through the trunk. In other words, the branches (you and I) are totally dependent upon Jesus for our spiritual sustenance and direction as Christians. No branch decides on its own what kind of fruit it will bear, or the shape of its leaves. All its instructions are received through the tree.

When a branch prays, he/she will not pray for anything that is contrary to the nature, character, and will of the vine/tree/Jesus. Jesus knows that if we remain in Him, we will only pray for things consistent with His will and character. That's why He said we can pray for anything we wish and it will be given to us. As our desires becomes consistent with His character and will, we won't ask selfishly for things contrary to the will of the Vine, and He will give us what we desire.

Chuckle: *While a woman was trying hard to get the ketchup out of its container, the phone rang. So she asked her 4-year-old daughter to answer the phone. "Mommy can't come to the phone right now. She's hitting the bottle."*

Quote: *"It is not faith and works; it is not faith or works; it is faith that works."* ~ Unknown Source

Grace, Faith, and Salvation

"For it is by grace you have been saved through faith—and this not from yourselves, it is the gift of God—not by works, so that no one can boast" (Ephesians 2:8-9 NIV).

The New Bible Dictionary says: *"Faith is the attitude whereby a person abandons all reliance in his own efforts to obtain salvation, be they deeds of piety, of ethical goodness or anything else. It is the attitude of complete trust in Christ, of reliance on him alone for all that salvation means."*

"What then shall we say? That the Gentiles, non-Jews, who did not pursue righteousness, have obtained it, a righteousness that is by faith; but Israel, who pursued a law of righteousness, has not attained it. Why not? Because they pursued it not by faith but as if it were by works" (Romans 9:30-32 NIV).

From the beginning, it has been God's intention for us to do good things for other people. However, we must understand that good works do not earn us a right standing with God. This can only come when we accept God's free gift of grace by placing our complete faith and trust in in Christ. Once we have placed our faith in Him, He makes us new creatures whose very nature is to do God's work. *"Therefore, if anyone is in Christ, he is a new creation; the old has gone, the new has come!"* (2 Corinthians 5:17 NIV).

Please take another look at the definition of faith above. There you will see that faith unto salvation is an attitude of total trust in Christ, and a reliance on Him alone. This faith leads to repentance of sin and acceptance of God's forgiveness. Once we have been born again and transformed by God's Holy Spirit, we will be motivated to work for Him through service to others. We will understand that *". . . we are God's workmanship (masterpiece), created in Christ Jesus to do good works, which God prepared in advance for us to do"* (Ephesians 2:10 NIV).

We become Christians through God's unmerited favor (grace)—not as a result of any effort, ability, or act of service on our part. Because our salvation, and even our faith, are gifts of God's grace, we should respond to Him with love, gratitude, praise, joy, and selfless acts of service.

May 28

Chuckle: *"Smartness runs in my family. When I went to school I was so smart my teacher was in my class for five years."*
~ George Burns

Quote: *"A house without a roof would scarcely be a more different home, than a family unsheltered by God's friendship, and the sense of being always rested in His providential care and guidance."*
~ Horace Bushnell

Family Fortune

"Give proper recognition to those widows who are really in need. But if a widow has children and grandchildren, these should learn first of all to put their religion into practice by caring for their own family and so repaying their parents and grandparents, for this is pleasing to God" (1 Timothy 5:3-4 NIV).

When you first saw the title of this lesson, what came to your mind? Was it the amount of money or possessions a family has accumulated? If so, I can understand your mind going in that direction. But let's give it a new meaning like: "my family is my fortune" or "how fortunate I am to have my family." As I grow older and come face to face with the reality that life is fragile and oh so brief, the fleeting time I have to spend with family becomes even more precious. Family members are my greatest fortune.

I'm reminded of a reunion in Casper, Wyoming, a few years ago. Gathered there were relatives from my grandmother's side of my family. As we laughed together, played together, shared memories together, and remembered those who are no longer with us, the preciousness of family was reinforced in many ways. As I looked into the faces of relatives whose lives are inextricably linked to mine, and whose lives have richly blessed my life, the beauty and value of family took on a fresh new meaning.

As I thought about our love for each other, I was reminded of God's amazing grace and love for each of us. He loves every member of my family, and yours, so much that He sacrificed His one and only Son to make it possible for our earthly families to experience the greatest reunion of all in heaven. And it will last for eternity. *"But God demonstrates his own love for us in this: While we were still sinners, Christ died for us"* (Romans 5:8 NIV).

Family is obviously the result of God's plan for human reproduction, but beyond that it fulfills the human desire for love and companionship. Family is also the setting within which our religious faith is nurtured through parental examples and teachings. Family is a symbol of God's relationship to His children as Father, as well as a symbol of the church in its relationship to Jesus Christ.

Family relationships do not remain strong automatically. They must be nurtured through love, Bible study, family worship, communication, conflict resolution, and friendships outside the family.

I hope you see your family as your greatest fortune, and I hope you never pass up an opportunity to let each one of them know how much you love and appreciate them. We never know when we will do so for the very last time in this life.

May 29

Chuckle: *"A young boy, ready for bed, interrupted a family gathering in the living room. 'I'm going up to say my prayers now. Anybody want anything?'"*

Quote: *"Acting is just a way to make a living, the family is life."* ~ Denzel Washington

Family of God

"So now you Gentiles are no longer strangers and foreigners. You are citizens along with God's holy people. You are members of God's family" (Ephesians 2:19 NLT). *"Whenever we have the opportunity, we should do good to everyone, especially to our Christian brothers and sisters"* (Galatians 6:10 NLT).

To me the word "family" is one of the most comforting words in the English language. On your walls, or in albums at home, you likely have pictures of both your immediate family members and those who have passed from the scene. Past or present, they are family. We inherited our physical characteristics from them—who we are.

In the same way our spiritual ancestors are a part of us. They formed the basis of who we are today. If you grew up in a Christian home where God's Word was taught and His love was modeled, you are blessed. Just take a moment and reflect on the beautiful memories of that wholesome family experience.

If you did not grow up in a Christian environment, but found Christ through the witness of another Christian, you can rejoice because a spiritual family member loved you and led you to Christ.

As I reflect on God's love for me and His adopting me into His eternal family through faith in Christ, a great joy and sense of gratitude wells up within me. God loves you and blesses you with His presence within you in the form of the Holy Spirit. You are further blessed to share in His family with all those within the church—your spiritual brothers and sisters who love you.

Let's think about what it means to be in God's family:

- It means we acknowledge that we belong to God. He created us and redeemed us through Jesus Christ. The belonging relationship is established.
- It means that it is God our Father who holds the family together through His Son who is the head of the church. When we recognize that we mutually and equally belong to God, it will bring harmony within His family.
- It means that only in this family can we grow to be what God wants us to be. As the child requires nurture and care in his earthly family, the new Christian needs spiritual nurturing and love to grow into the family member God desires.
- It means we rejoice at the birth of a new member. When we get the news that a baby has been born, we joyfully spread the word to every family member.

Likewise the church, entrusted with the good news of salvation, proclaims with joy the gospel of forgiveness. We rejoice when a new believer is "born again" into God's family and our local church fellowship, and when missionaries tell us of spiritual births in distant lands.

May 30

Chuckle: *"A little boy had a part in the school play that read, 'It is I; be not afraid.' He came out on the stage and said, 'It's me and I'm scared!'"*

Quote: *"I sought the LORD, and he answered me; he delivered me from all my fears"* (Psalm 34:4 NIV).

Living Without Fear

"Fear not, for I have <u>redeemed</u> you; I have summoned you by name; you are mine. . . When you pass through the waters, <u>I will be with you</u>. . . You are precious and honored in my sight, and <u>I love you</u>" (Isaiah 43:1-5 NIV).

Webster defines "fear" as: *"That strong sense of personal danger whether real or imagined."* There are many kinds of fears today:

- Physical fears (cancer and other illnesses);
- Financial fears (bills, losing job, etc.);
- Future fears (divorce, aloneness, etc.);
- Family fears (for children, parents, etc);
- Fear of rejection;
- Fear of the unknown

...FEAR!

Both non-Christians and Christians alike can have fears. But God does not want His children to be afraid. God has a message of assurance that will calm your fears and restore peace and contentment to your life. Our passage gives three primary reasons why you should not fear.

First, God has <u>redeemed you</u>. To redeem means to buy someone out of slavery. God delivered the Hebrew people from over 400 years (1700-1300 B.C.) of physical slavery in Egypt. Even more miraculous is the truth that God has redeemed you from the slavery of sin by the blood of Jesus, and delivered you from the fear of spending eternity separated from His presence. *"For you know that it was not with perishable things such as silver and gold that you were redeemed . . . . but with the precious blood of Christ, a lamb without blemish or defect"*(1 Pet. 1:18 NIV).

Second, God says "I am with you." In all of life's trials, He is with us. In verse 2, God says "when"—not "if"— you pass through troubled times (waters, rivers, storms, fires, trials, problems). As your Savior, Christ is always with you. *"He tends his flock like a shepherd: He gathers the lambs in his arms and carries them close to his heart"* (Isaiah 40:11 NIV). *"Never will I leave you; never will I forsake you. So we can say with confidence, the Lord is my helper; I will not be afraid"* (Heb. 13:5-6 NIV).

Third, God loves you. He says, *"You are precious and honored in my sight, and I love you."* The King of the universe thinks you are well worth His Son dying for you. You're precious to Him—valuable and rare. You're honored, which means you carry weight with God. *"Cast all your anxieties on Him because He cares for you"* (1 Peter 5:7 NIV).

To see how much God loves you, just substitute your name for "the world" in John 3:16. Jesus loves you unconditionally just the way you are. Max Lucado put it this way: *If God carried a wallet, your picture would be in it.* God will not abandon you because He loves you.

If you have Christ as Savior, you need not be afraid. You and I can say with the psalmist, *"When I'm afraid, I will trust in you. In God whose word I praise, in God I trust; I will never be afraid, what can mortal man do to me?"* (Psalm 56:3 NIV).

May 31

Chuckle: *"I'm seventy five years old. Forget about the health food . . . I need all the preservatives I can get!"*

Quote: *"Jesus is the only one who can bring us to forgiveness. He waits for us to turn our hearts over to him; then he performs the healing, changing, finishing miracles."* ~ Holly Metcalf

God Gives Second Chances

"Then the word of the Lord came to Jonah a second time: 'Go to the great city of Nineveh and proclaim to it the message I give you.'" (Jonah 3:1-2 NIV).

I'm sure you remember the account of a prophet of God named Jonah. God told him to go and preach to the wicked people of Nineveh—cruel arch-enemies of Israel.

Jonah refused and ran from God in the opposite direction from Nineveh. As he sailed from Joppa toward a city called Tarshish, he was thrown overboard to save the ship in a violent storm and was swallowed by a giant fish. It was inside the fish that Jonah repented and God gave him a second chance by having the fish deposit him on dry land. Jonah did as God had commanded and the people of Nineveh repented.

You may remember how Simon Peter denied Jesus on the night Jesus was arrested. He swore that he did not even know Jesus. Jesus had predicted his denial even when Peter said he would never do such a thing. Peter denied Jesus three times during the night before the rooster crowed as Jesus had predicted. The Bible says when Peter heard the rooster, he went out and wept bitterly. But Jesus forgave him and gave him another chance. Peter didn't blow it this time, and he became one of the early stalwarts of the Christian faith.

Most of us can vouch for the fact that we serve a God of second chances—or maybe third, fourth, or fifth chances. You may have disobeyed God, wandered away from Him and His church, and are living as if you don't even know Jesus. If so, you may be thinking that God will give up on you and will not forgive you. But that's not the way the heart of God works. He loves you and, like a shepherd searching for a wandering sheep or a father searching for his prodigal son, will welcome you back into the fold of His fellowship and His church.

It is by God's grace, love, and mercy that He grants wayward Christians second chances. The Bible says, *"I urge you not to receive God's grace in vain"* (2 Corinthians 6:1 NIV). Do not reject God's invitation to re-join Him in His kingdom work.

In other words, don't blow it again when God gives you a second chance. But jump at the chance to repent of your sins and once again feel the warmth and security of God's love and forgiveness, and enjoy the fellowship with God's people.

Jun 01

Chuckle: *"Insomnia is contagious; if your baby has it, chances are you will have it too!!"*

Quote: *"If his conditions are met, God is bound by his Word to forgive any man or woman of any sin because of Christ."* ~ Billy Graham

New Heart, New Spirit, New Nature

"Now turn from your sins and turn to God, so you can be cleansed of your sins" (Acts 3:19 NLT). *"And I will give you a new heart with new and right desires, and I will put a new spirit in you. I will take out your stony heart of sin and give you a new, obedient heart. And I will put my Spirit in you so you will obey my laws and do whatever I command"* (Ezekiel 36:26-27 NLT).

God has a plan for the life of every human being. God had Ezekiel record for us an Old Testament image of the New Testament plan of salvation through faith in Christ.

When we place our faith in Jesus as our personal Lord and Savior, God, through His Spirit, creates within us a new nature. *". . . you have clothed yourselves with a brand-new nature that is continually being renewed as you learn more and more about Christ, who created this new nature within you"* (Colossians 3:10 NLT). In each Christian, there is a continuous battle between the old sinful nature and the new nature God has given us.

"So I advise you to live according to your new life in the Holy Spirit. Then you won't be doing what your sinful nature craves. The old sinful nature loves to do evil, which is just opposite from what the Holy Spirit wants. And the Spirit gives us desires that are opposite from what the sinful nature desires. The

*two forces are constantly fighting each other, and your choices
are never free from this conflict"* (Galatians 5:16-17 NLT).

Over the course of time, the way we live is dependent
upon which nature we choose to give control over our lives. If
the old nature wins, we will drift away from God and the joy of
a daily walk and fellowship with Him. When this happens, we
lose interest in attending church. We stop studying God's
Word. We stop praying. And we stop enjoying the fellowship of
other Christians.

If you find yourself in this situation, you need a renewal
of commitment to God. You need revival. You may need to pray
as did the psalmist: *"Create in me a clean heart, O God. Renew a
right spirit within me"* (Psalm 51:10 NLT).

Every Christian can claim the promise of 1 John 1:9,
*"But if we confess our sins to him, he is faithful and just to forgive
us and to cleanse us from every wrong."* By admitting our sins
and receiving Christ's cleansing, we are agreeing with God that
our sin is truly sin and that we are willing to turn away from it.
We are ensuring that we don't try to conceal our sins from Him
and consequently, from ourselves. We are recognizing our
tendency to sin, and we begin relying on His power to help us
overcome it.

Gipsy Smith, the celebrated English evangelist of an
earlier time, gave these instructions for repentance and
revival: "Go to a quiet place to pray. With a piece of chalk and
draw a circle completely around yourself. Then pray for God to
send revival to everyone in the circle. Stay there until God
answers —and then you will have revival."

Jun 02

Chuckle: *"While visiting a police station, a kindergartener pointed to a picture and asked if the photo was of a wanted person. "Yes," answered a policeman.*

"Well," asked the child, "why didn't you keep him when you took his picture?"

Quote: *"See the Gospel Church secure And founded on a Rock! All her promises are sure; Her bulwarks who can shock?*
~ Charles Wesley 'The Church'

Working Together

"From him the whole body joined and held together by every supporting ligament, grows and builds itself up in love, as each part does its work" (Ephesians 4:16 NIV). *"The body is a unit, though it is made up of many parts; and though all its parts are many, they form one body"* (1 Corinthians 12:12 NIV).

You are probably familiar with the word "synergy" and "synergism." Synergy says: "the function of the whole is greater than the sum of its individual parts."

For example, you can have all the parts of a clock spread out on a table, but just having all the parts does not make a clock. It becomes a functioning clock only when the cooperating parts are assembled and perform their intended functions as they work together. The clock is greater than the sum of its parts.

Synergism also describes different medicines working together to produce the desired healing effect.

The word "synergism" is also used in a theological sense: "It is the doctrine or belief that the human will cooperates with the Holy Spirit and with God's grace especially in the act of conversion or regeneration." God's grace, the Holy Spirit's power, and the faith of the individual are all at work together. *"For it is by grace you have been saved, through faith"* (Ephesians 2:8 NIV).

Jesus Christ, the head of the church, desires every born again Christian to be an active member of His universal church through local congregations. There is definitely a Holy Spirit empowered and directed synergy when Christians are working together as a fellowship of believers—the church. The church, consisting of many members, has been commissioned by Christ to do His work here on earth until He returns.

A church, with all is members working together in the power of the Holy Spirit, creates a powerful synergy to accomplish much more than the same number of individual Christians going it alone without the church. The Holy Spirit empowers church members, and uses their spiritual gifts and interdependency to create spiritual synergy within the church.

If you profess to be a Christian, but are not affiliated with a local church, I urge you become involved with a Bible believing congregation and put your God-given skills and spiritual gifts to work as a member of the whole. The same is true for church members who do not actively participate in the five functions of the church: worship, evangelism, discipleship, ministry, and fellowship.

The Church is the Body of Christ, with Christ as its head. Like the human body, the church cannot function as Christ intended unless all members are working together and performing their specific functions within the body.

Jun 03

Chuckle: *I've started a new exercise program. As I wake each morning, I always say sternly to myself, "Ready? Now up and down, up, down." After two strenuous minutes I tell myself, "OK, now let's try the other eyelid!"*

Quote: *"Not teaching your son the value of hard work is like teaching him to steal."* ~ Unknown Source

The Value of Hard Work

"Work hard and cheerfully at whatever you do, as though you were working for the Lord rather than for people" (Colossians 3:23 NLT).

It seems to me that in the past much more of people's self-esteem came from the quality of their work—their pride and joy. Whatever they did, they wanted to give it their best effort so that their work would reflect positively not only on their abilities and skills, but more importantly, on their character. Pride in our work should be a major source of satisfaction in our lives. It is dangerous to generalize, but it seems many of us have lost much of what was once a respected work ethic.

In my own life, I have observed many who did not care how well they did their work as long as they received a pay check. They did just enough to get by, but were not overly concerned about what people might think of them and the quality of their work as long as they did enough not to get fired. This should never be the attitude of a Christian.

We are to be Christ's representatives wherever we are and whatever we are doing. That includes our workplace. We should be the most dependable, productive, and pleasant workers around as we honor our Lord with our labor.

It has been God's plan from creation that we should work in order to provide for ourselves and our families. God's word has much to say about the value of work and the destructive nature of laziness. *"If anyone does not provide for his relatives, and especially for his immediate family, he has denied the faith and is worse than an unbeliever"* (1 Timothy 5:8 NIV). *"If a man will not work, he shall not eat"* (2 Thessalonians 3:10b NIV).

If we could see our work as an act of worship and service to our Lord, our whole attitude about work would change. It would take the drudgery out of our toil, give us greater self-satisfaction, increase our productivity, and give us greater joy.

Here Paul is admonishing slaves to work hard in order to please their masters—to work as if they are working for their Lord. Paul is not advocating slavery, but is making the point that our work should always be given the best of our abilities.

Although Paul was talking about working for earthly masters, the same principles apply when working for the Master, our Lord Himself. We should pray for God to bless the work of our hands and mind. And we should work wholeheartedly to bring glory to our Lord as we reveal Him to others by our character as shown through our work ethic.

Jun 04

Chuckle: *Mother: "Tommy, why did you kick your sister in the stomach?*

Tommy: "I couldn't help it. She turned around too quick!"

Quote: *"Good words are worth much, and cost little."*
~ George Herbert

Words Reveal Our Hearts

"With the tongue we praise our Lord and Father, and with it we curse men (people), who have been made in God's likeness. Out of the same mouth come praise and cursing" (James 3:9-10 NIV).

By and large, each of us is the product of our childhood environment and upbringing. If we grew up in a home and community where people of a different race or ethnicity were looked down upon and demeaned by our parents, or others with whom we associated, prejudicial feelings may have become deeply rooted in our hearts and minds. If so, it may be difficult for us to change our attitude and begin accepting all people, and recognizing that God loves them in the same way He loves us.

"If you, . . . 'Love your neighbor as yourself,' you are doing right. But if you show favoritism, you sin and are convicted by the law as lawbreakers" (James 2:8-9 NIV).

Who we really are will be revealed by the words we speak. Harboring prejudices, biases, and favoritisms may result in the habitual use of disrespectful and hurtful language. We may try to convince others that we have no prejudices, but our words will communicate otherwise.

It could be that the use of prejudicial and unkind words

has become a permanent part of a person's everyday vocabulary. If so, that person may be using offensive language without even realizing the damage he or she is inflicting on others. But make no mistake, our words reveal our true identity.

Even if we don't intend to hurt anyone by what we say, our manner of speaking can do irreparable harm to our relationships with other people. If you make disparaging remarks about a specific individual, your relationship with that person will be damaged. However, your words may also be offensive to others who do not share your racial or ethnic prejudices and do not approve of racially charged language.

If we truly know Jesus Christ as Savior and Lord, our desire will be to see all people through His eyes and love everyone as He loves them. If we love as Jesus loves, we—with God's help—will make a determined effort to treat everyone with the same love, courtesy, and respect. We will intentionally guard our tongues and evaluate every word we utter to be sure we are honoring our Lord and edifying other people. If we harbor prejudicial feelings, sooner or later our words will reveal the depth of those feelings.

"If anyone considers himself religious and yet does not keep a tight rein on his tongue, he deceives himself and his religion is worthless" (James 2:1 NIV). The good news is that God wants to change us from the inside out. When our hearts have been purified by the Holy Spirit, our views of others will change and so will our words.

Jun 05

Chuckle: *"Why is it that you always find what you're looking for in the last place you look? Because you stop looking for it after you find it."*

Quote: *"Whenever the insistence is on the point that God answers prayer, we are off the track. The meaning of prayer is that we get hold of God, not the answer."* ~ Oswald Chambers

Valuables with Eternal Value

"He who pursues righteousness and love finds life, prosperity, and honor" (Proverbs 21:21 NIV). *"Seek first his (God's) kingdom and his righteousness, and all these things will be given to you as well"* (Matthew 6:32 NIV).

Each of us will approach God in our own way to gain understanding of the values He would have us assimilate into our hearts and lives. However, here is a simple set of steps that may help guide you toward that end:

- Focus on the valuable. *"For the ear tests words as the tongue tastes food. Let us discern for ourselves what is right; let us learn together what is good"* (Job 34:3 NIV). Have you determined what is right, good, and important for your life? Rich or poor, you can have the joy of knowing you're living by values that are important to God. Don't be deceived by the world's values, but seek God's values. Write down what's most important to you—your valuables. Will they last?
- Discard the valueless. This is elementary, but so important. *"Turn my eyes away from worthless things; preserve my life according to your Word"*

(Psalm 119:37 NIV). You begin to give God His place when you say: "My family members are important and I will spend time with them." "I will wisely spend the money God has given me for Him and my family." "I will guide and teach my family in spiritual matters." Eliminate anything that does not build relationships with God and other people. You can't add God's priorities to a life already filled and stressed to the max with other time-consuming and less important activities. Time for prayer, Bible study, family, church, etc. must replace something in a busy life.

- Focus on the eternal. What lasts? What matters? What continues? *"And now these three things remain: faith, hope, and love"* (1 Corinthians 13:13 NIV). If you love God and people, and make them your priorities, you're building a life of eternal value. If you have a strong and growing faith in Jesus Christ, you have discovered what is important. You will win at life! The test of your faith is how important other people are to you.

What is most important in your life? You have two options: the world's values or God's values. Which appeals to you the most? To which set of values is your heart drawn?

Sadly, *"Some have missed the most important thing— they don't know God"* (1 Timothy 6:21 NIV). If you don't know Jesus Christ as Savior, just open your heart to Him and by faith claim the most valuable gift of all time. *"Everything else is worthless compared to the surpassing greatness of knowing Christ Jesus my Lord..."* (Philippians 3:8 NIV).

Chuckle: *"Why do croutons come in airtight packages? It's just stale bread to begin with."*

Quote: *"Each man decides whether he will be engulfed by the urgent, engrossed by the trivial, or enriched by the eternal."* ~ William Arthur Ward

Trying to Serve Two Masters

"No one can serve two masters. For you will hate one and love the other, or be devoted to one and despise the other. You cannot serve both God and money" (Matthew 6:24 NLT).

As Christians, we have no choice but to live in a society where many people worship and serve money. Christians are certainly not immune to adopting this worldly view. Many spend their entire lives accumulating and storing money and possessions, only to die and leave it all behind. I've never seen a hearse pulling a U-Haul trailer, have you? Unfortunately, the commitment of many to money and what it can buy far outweighs their commitment to God and spiritual matters.

Can you honestly say that God, and not money, is your master? Whatever you store up, you will spend much of your time and energy thinking about, fretting about, and planning how to accumulate more.

Are the choices you make based on materialism? *"Let your character be free from the love of money..."* (Hebrews 13:5).

"For the love of money is at the root of all kinds of evil. And some people, craving money, have wandered away from the faith, and pierced themselves with many sorrows" (1 Timothy 6:10 NLT). This passage is often misquoted. It is not money that is the problem—it is our infatuation with it. It is making it our

master.

God's Word encourages hard work and good management to provide for our families. Having possessions, or not, is not the issue. It is our attitudes toward them. We are either serving God or serving money. If we are serving money, we are allowing it, instead of the Holy Spirit, to control us as we worship and serve God as our Master. We can become possessed by our possessions. An easy test is to ask yourself this question: "Which occupies more of my thoughts, time, and efforts—God or money?"

In the teachings of Jesus, He often contrasted heavenly values with earthly values. He explains that our first loyalty should be to those things that do not fade, cannot be stolen or used up, and never wear out. *"Store your treasures in heaven, where they will never become moth-eaten or rusty and where they will be safe from thieves. Wherever your treasure is, there your heart and thoughts will be"* (Matthew 6:20-21 NLT). If money and possessions are becoming too important to us, we should evaluate our walk with God.

In our basic passage, Jesus asks us to make a choice—to serve Him or to serve material things. If we choose to truly make Him the Master of our lives, He will teach us to be content with whatever we have because we have chosen that which has eternal value. He also promises to supply what we need if we make Him our first priority (see Matthew 6:33).

Jun 07

Chuckle: *"Old aunts used to come up to me at weddings, poke me in the ribs and cackle, "You're next!" They stopped after I started doing the same thing to them—at funerals!*

Quote: *"Conquer a man who never gives by gifts; Subdue untruthful men by truthfulness; Vanquish an angry man by gentleness; And overcome the evil man by goodness."*
~ Unknown Source

Living Truthfully

"The Lord detests lying lips, but he delights in men who are truthful" (Proverbs 12:22 NIV). *"Good people are guided by their honesty; treacherous people are destroyed by their dishonesty"* (Proverbs 11:3 NLT).

Sometime back I was watching a golf tournament on TV. The commentators were discussing a young player, Brian Davis, who had voluntarily penalized himself two shots for inadvertently moving a reed on his back-swing prior to taking a shot from the rough. The violation of rule 13.4 against moving a loose impediment during a takeaway was indiscernible but for slow motion replays.

No one saw the reed move. He could have taken the shot as if the infraction had never occurred, and no one would have been the wiser. But his personal code of conduct would not allow him to do so. He said he could not have lived with himself if he had not reported the infraction.

When thinking about living truthfully, it's easy to justify untruthful conduct as long as we know nobody's watching. If the fear of getting caught motivates us to be truthful, then we aren't truthful at all. We are masquerading. We are being hypocritical. We are not what we want others to think we are.

Truthfulness comes from a set of character values deep within us that are more important to us than the possible rewards being untruthful might bring—like a chance to win your first PGA golf tournament with its million-dollar pay check.

It should be our desire to live pure and holy lives before both God and other people. There is a definite relationship between living truthfully and living a holy life.

"The relationship between truth and holiness is similar to that between light and vision. Light cannot create an eye or give a blind eye vision, but it is essential to seeing. Wherever light penetrates, it dissipates darkness and brings everything into view. In a similar manner, truth cannot regenerate or impart spiritual life, but it is essential to the practice of holiness. Wherever truth penetrates, it dissipates error and reveals everything for what it really is." ~ *Illustrations for Biblical Preaching*, Edited by Michael P. Green

Dishonesty, in words and actions, is the opposite of what God expects and honors, and honesty is more than just verbally telling the truth. It is living with integrity not only in what we say but in what we do. If we want to please God and enjoy the respect of others, like the young golf pro has done, we will live truthfully in all circumstances.

Jun 08

Chuckle: *A man sat in the pew, scratching and scratching. Finally, the minister stopped his sermon and asked, "Why are you scratching like that?"*

The man replied, "Cause I'm the only one who knows where I itch!"

Quote: *"The inward stirring and touching of God makes us hungry and yearning; for the Spirit of God hurts our spirit; and the more he touches it, the greater our hunger and craving."* ~ Jan van Ruysbroeck

Thirst for Living Water

"On the last day, the climax of the festival, Jesus stood and shouted to the crowds, 'If you are thirsty, come to me! If you believe in me, come and drink! For the Scriptures declare that rivers of living water will flow out from within.' When he said, 'living water,' he was speaking of the Spirit, who would be given to everyone believing in him" (John 7:37-39a NLT). *"Blessed are those who hunger and thirst for righteousness, for they will be filled"* (Matthew 5:6 NIV).

Do you have a deep and sincere craving or thirst for the Holy Spirit to fill your life? The Spirit-filled life begins with a thirst that nothing else can quench—a desire growing out of discontentment with our current spiritual condition. This discontentment grows into a deep longing for a life filled with the Spirit. This is the first step toward experiencing the abundant flow and overflow of the "streams of living water."

When Jesus used the words "come and drink," He was alluding to the theme of many Bible passages that make reference to the Messiah's life-giving blessings. By promising to give the Holy Spirit to all who believed, Jesus was putting forth His claim that He was the promised Messiah. No one except the Messiah could make good on such an offer.

In John 4:10, Jesus spoke of "living water" to indicate eternal life. But here He uses it to refer to the Holy Spirit. Of course, this double usage makes sense because, for whomever accepts the Holy Spirit, the Spirit brings eternal life. Jesus taught us much about the Holy Spirit, and then the Spirit empowered Jesus' followers at Pentecost. Down through the ages since that time, the Spirit has been available and resident in everyone who believes in Jesus as Savior.

When your thirst allows the Spirit to fill your life, you are taught, convicted, comforted, and led by Him in every aspect of your life. In other words, you are filled with the Spirit each day. Your thirst is quenched and you experience the power and peace of God in everything you do.

How about you? Do you have that thirst about which Jesus was teaching? If so, you will not be disappointed.

These words by J. S. Baxter describe God's plan for His Holy Spirit in your life: "What God chooses, He cleanses. What God cleanses, He molds. What God molds, He fills. What God fills, He uses."

Jun 09

Chuckle: *My Mother-in Law is a master of the mixed metaphor. One day in Sunday school she outdid herself when she warned her students' parents that if they didn't teach their children properly, "their roosters would come home to croak."*
~ Tod Smith

Quote: *"In His love He clothes us, enfolds and embraces us; that tender love completely surrounds us, never to leave us."*
~ Julian of Norwich

The Open Door

Jesus to the church at Philadelphia: *"I know all the things you do, and I have opened a door for you that no one can shut. You have little strength, yet you obeyed my word and did not deny me"* (Revelation 3:8 NLT).

Think with me for a moment about this amazing truth. As a devoted follower of Christ, God has provided a door for you into His very presence, in the name of Jesus, which no power can ever close. No one can exclude you from God's kingdom. You can never be shut out.

An open door into our homes and the presence of our families who love us gives us a sense of peace, comfort, and acceptance. A door into God's presence is far and away more significant and reassuring because it has eternal implications.

I remember some years ago, a motel chain made famous the comforting phrase, "We'll leave the light on for you." The voice of Tom Bodett had a slow, folksy, down home quality that assured weary travelers that the door to a clean and comfortable room would always be open for them any time of day or night. Incidentally, on its 50th anniversary, the motel chain began using the phrase: "50 years—the light is still on."

In this life, God fully understands that we are weak and weary travelers. But He encourages us by assuring us of the availability of His strength and protection when we obey His Word and are faithful in proclaiming His name. God opens the door into His presence and into His future kingdom. And after the door is opened, it will never be closed. No one can ever close it—our salvation is certain.

The comforting words of Jesus, in our passage, assure us that our place in God's kingdom and presence has been eternally reserved and sealed. Jesus is now preparing a place for us in His eternal heaven—a place of complete joy and peace. This is all because of God's never ending love for us.

"For I am convinced that neither death nor life, neither angels or demons, neither the present or the future, not any powers, neither height nor depth, nor anything else in all creation, will be able to separate us from the love of God that is in Christ Jesus our Lord" (Romans 8:38-39 NIV).

Jun 10

Chuckle: *Just think how much deeper the ocean would be if sponges didn't live there!!*

Quote: *"I never knew how to worship until I knew how to love."* ~ Henry Ward Beecher

The Main Thing

The Greatest Commandment: *"Love the Lord your God with all your heart and with all your soul and with all your mind and with all your strength"* (Mark 12:30 NIV).

A few years back—here in Texas—we had an outstanding evangelism leader who always encouraged Christians to "keep the main thing the main thing." In our passage, Jesus tells us, in no uncertain terms, what the main thing is.

When Jesus was asked what was the most important commandment, He did not hesitate to give us the Great Commandment. Love is the heart of the Christian life—like the old hymn: "Love is the Theme; love is supreme. . ." And the most important thing for us is our love for God because our ability to love others depends upon our love for our Lord.

But let's not forget that knowing the Great Commandment and living it out are two different things. If we do in fact love God according to the Great Commandment, the first indication will be our joyful obedience to His other commands and instructions, which includes loving others. You cannot love God and continue to do as you like. You cannot love God and disobey Him. Jesus said, *"If anyone loves me, he will obey my teaching"* (John 14:23 NIV).

If you say you love God but do not obey Him, you do not

love Him the way the Great Commandment describes. If our love for God is not complete, then trying to be obedient becomes burdensome, unpleasant, and futile. True love for our Lord expresses itself in sincere worship and joyful obedience.

Immediately following the Great Commandment, Jesus said, *"The second (greatest commandment) is this: Love your neighbor as yourself. There is no greater commandment than these"* (Mark 12:31 NIV). If we first love God with all our hearts, we will gladly obey Him by loving others as God has loved us. Even John 3:16 is all about God's love for us—the most powerful force in all creation. If we combine the Great Commandment with the Great Commission in Matthew 28:19-20, we have our spiritual marching orders as believers. We are to love God, love others, and share the gospel message of Jesus Christ.

Listen to these words: *"My beloved friends, let us continue to love each other since love comes from God. Everyone who loves is born of God and experiences a relationship with God. The person who refuses to love doesn't know the first thing about God, because God is love—so you can't know him if you don't love"* (1 John 4:7-8 MSG).

Enough said.

Jun 11

Chuckle: *A speeding driver was pulled over. The driver asked, "Why was I pulled over when I wasn't the only one speeding?"*
The policeman replied, "Have you ever been fishing?"
"Yes," answered the motorist.
"And have you ever caught all the fish?"
Quote: *". . . They always talk who never think."*
~ Matthew Prior

Bluffing Is Bad

"Everyone should be quick to listen, slow to speak and slow to become angry,.." (James 1:19b NIV). *"When words are many, sin is not absent, but he who holds his tongue is wise"* (Proverbs 10:19 NIV).

Have you ever tried to bluff your way through a conversation by talking in an attempt to hide your ignorance about the subject. Pride is a terrible, powerful, and destructive force within us. Pride tells us it is a sign of weakness to admit we are wrong, or less informed than someone else.

Have you ever come to the conclusion that you were wrong about something, but you kept on arguing your position anyway? I'm reminded of a saying I heard as a boy: "You would argue with a road sign and then take the wrong road."

When we try to bluff our way through an embarrassing situation by talking rather than listening, we will lose credibility and feel shame, guilt, and regret in the long run.

Because of pride, we feel compelled to look better and more important than someone else. Confessing ignorance is difficult for the proud person, but real strength is displayed when we swallow our pride, listen carefully, and confess that we don't have all the answers. Constant, meaningless, thoughtless, and offensive chatter may be an effort to hide a lack of ability, knowledge, or confidence. The following should teach each of us a valuable lesson:

Once, while crossing the Atlantic, an editor was approached by a fellow passenger. "I just wanted to tell you" the man said, and it was obvious he was speaking with considerable emotion, "how deeply I appreciated your message."

Now, the editor could not recall the occasion for any message; in fact he could not even place the man who seemed so grateful. <u>But rather than admit he was at a loss</u>, he said rather grandly: "Oh, that's all right. I was glad for the opportunity to send it."

Naturally, he was puzzled when the other man turned absolutely white and left abruptly without another word.

On making discreet inquiries, the old editor confessed, "I learned that I knew the man, indeed, and that the message I had been 'so glad to send' him had been one of condolence on the recent death of his wife!" ~ Sidney Shalett

We can avoid such blunders and embarrassments by being quick to listen and slow to speak—by thinking first, and then speaking only after we understand what the other person is saying, and carefully considering the impact of our words on the other person.

Jun 12

Chuckle: *"God does not believe in atheists; therefore atheists do not exist."*

Quote: *"A man who loses his conscience has nothing left that is worth keeping."* ~ Izaak Walton

The Consciences Within Us

"So I strive always to keep my conscience clear before God and man" (Acts 24:16 NIV). *"I speak the truth in Christ— I am not lying, my conscience confirms it in the Holy Spirit"* (Romans 9:1 NIV).

"A mother was helping her son with his spelling assignment and came to the words 'conscious and 'conscience.' When she asked him if he knew the difference between the two, he responded, 'Sure, Mom, 'conscious' is when you are aware of something and 'conscience' is when you wish your weren't.'"

The human conscience is a complex subject indeed. We often hear such statements as: "Let your conscience be your guide;" "My conscience is clear;" "I did it with a clear conscience;" "I can sleep well at night;" or "My conscience is bothering me." Sometimes we see someone do a terrible thing and we react with: "Don't you have a conscience?"

In Scripture, the word for conscience is *"that faculty by which we apprehend the will of God, as that which is designed to govern our lives."* Hence we feel a sense of guiltiness before God when we sin against him. The Holy Spirit guides the Christian conscience in knowledge and emotion.

The Spirit-controlled conscience of Christians results in a thought process which distinguishes between the morally good and bad, commending the good, condemning the bad, and prompting us to do the good and avoid the bad. As we grow in our faith, our consciences become progressively more sensitive to the will of God. If you have occasion to question whether an action is right or wrong, it's probably wrong in God's sight. Otherwise, your conscience would have allowed you to do it without question.

Have you ever done something after having rationalized that it was not a sin, but you felt a sense of guilt from having done it anyway. As a Christian, when you sin against another person or against God, you will have this miserable feeling of guilt and sorrow. That's because your conscience is being influenced by the Holy Spirit that dwells within you, and is being sensitized to even the nuances of right and wrong.

As you allow the Spirit to control your life, your conscience will become increasingly reliable as your moral guide. It could be said that God's Word and the Holy Spirit become the conscience of a Christian.

Jun 13

Chuckle: *The customer called the waiter over and said, while pointing to his steak, "Didn't I tell you, 'Well done'?"*

The waiter replied, "Thank you, Sir; I seldom get a compliment."

Quote: *"Conscience is that faculty in me which attaches itself to the highest that I know, and tells me what the highest I know demands that I do."* ~ Oswald Chambers

The Searing of Conscience

"Such teachings come through hypocritical liars, whose consciences have been seared with a hot iron" (1 Timothy 4:2 NIV). *"Having lost all sensitivity, they have given themselves over to sensuality so as to indulge in every kind of impurity, with a continual lust for more"* (Ephesians 4:19 NIV).

Last time, we saw how living Spirit-controlled lives will sensitize our consciences to detect even the most minute breach in our moral and ethical standard of conduct. We saw that Paul was striving to have a clear conscience before God and before people. In our Scripture passages for today, we see that our consciences can become seared, dulled, and unreliable as guides for our lives. How can our consciences become "seared?" In the simplest terms—SIN!

"The conscience is like a sharp square peg in our hearts. If we are confronted by a questionable situation, that square begins to turn and it's corners cut into our hearts, warning us with an inward sensation against doing whatever confronts us. If the conscience is ignored time after time, the corners of the square are gradually worn down, and it virtually becomes a circle. When that circle turns within our hearts, there is no inner sensation of warning, and we are left without a conscience." ~ *Illustrations for Biblical Preaching;* Edited by Michael P. Green

If we allow unconfessed and unforgiven sin to become prevalent in our lives and compromise, our consciences will lose their sensitivity to right and wrong. This will gradually render us spiritually undiscerning—unable to discern what is right from what is wrong. Eventually our consciences will become useless. We begin to live a life of disobedience and sin without the pangs of conscience we once felt. I believe this explains why some professed "Christians" can indulge in the most destructive, hurtful, and immoral behavior with, seemingly, no remorse or regret. The more we sin, the more our consciences are disabled. The "hot iron" of sin has "seared" our consciences and hardened our hearts against the Holy Spirit.

The positive side of all this is that the Spirit can—and will—provide our consciences with very definite and reliable guidance if only we allow him to do so. The Spirit-filled life is the Spirit-controlled life. The Spirit-controlled life will be led by a Spirit-controlled conscience.

Whatever sin is in your life that interferes with your inner communion with God, confess it, ask forgiveness for it, and let it go so that your inner vision from God—your conscience—will remain clear and crisp.

Jun 14

Chuckle: *Thomas Edison's Mother: "Of course I'm proud that you invented the electric light bulb. Now turn it off and go to bed!"*

Quote: *"Trust that man in nothing who has not a conscience in everything."* ~ Laurence Sterne

The Consciences of the Unsaved

"How much more, then, will the blood of Christ, who through the eternal Spirit offered himself unblemished to God, cleanse our consciences from acts that lead to death, so that we may serve the living God" (Hebrews 9:14 NIV).

We often observe criminal activity where the offender shows no pangs of conscience or remorse. We marvel at such out-of-control lives, and the obvious, total disregard for the welfare of others. One truth is patently clear—unless a person's conscience is adequately trained and sensitized, it is useless as a moral guide for human conduct. Our consciences will be trained by the secular morality of the world, or by the morality of God's Word and the Holy Spirit.

Before we become Christians, our consciences are trained by the definitions of right and wrong that we have been taught in the home, school, and other life-shaping venues. Unfortunately, all too many children grow up in homes where parents have no moral compass. These children will, in turn, contribute to a society with no moral absolutes—seemingly without conscience. This is the "if it feels good, do it" generation. Right and wrong become relative terms and their definitions depend upon the situation at the time. The conscience of a non-Christian is missing the key factor for a conscience that will lead to conduct that pleases God and glorifies Him through one's relationships with others. The unsaved conscience has no concept of what it means to live one's life with the sole purpose of pleasing God.

You may say, "But, Jerry, I know a lot of people who are not Christians who live good, clean, moral lives—how do you explain that?"

You're right. I have also made such observations, and we should be thankful for such people. Some non-Christian homes produce children who live moral lives. They make a huge difference in alleviating human suffering, and their kindnesses are extremely beneficial to our society. However, none of what they do will lead to their eternal salvation or gain them any status in the eyes of God. Without Christ, they are still lost and without hope.

You see, when our consciences are being shaped and ruled by the Holy Spirit, we will not only do good deeds and live a morally upright life, but the very motives for our actions will also be controlled by the Spirit. When we live by a Spirit-controlled conscience, we please and honor God. *"The Lord's searchlight penetrates the human spirit, exposing every hidden motive"* (Proverbs 20:27 NIV).

In our Hebrews passage, we see that only the blood of Christ can cleanse and purify our consciences so we no longer make decisions that can lead to our spiritual death. These include depending on a good life to earn God's favor and assure us a place in heaven.

Jun 15

Chuckle: *Counterfeiters (kown'-ter-fit'-ers): Workers who put together kitchen cabinets.*

Quote: *"Courage is not simply one of the virtues, but the form of every virtue at the testing point, which means at the point of highest reality."* ~ C.S. Lewis Quoted Cyril Connolly

Courageous Christians

"Be on guard. Stand true to what you believe. Be courageous. Be strong. And everything you do must be done with love" (1 Corinthians 16:13 NLT).

The dictionary defines courage as "being able to control one's fear and so to face danger, pain, or trouble willingly; bravery."

Here Paul encourages the Corinthians to be alert and on guard against spiritual adversaries and the danger they represent. He reminds them to stand firm in their faith, and to be courageous and strong, showing kindness and love in all their interpersonal relationships. These words of encouragement are badly needed by Christians today.

It seems that every day brings another threat to our peace of mind and sense of well-being. If it isn't international terror, it's domestic crime in the form of identity theft, car-jacking, home invasions, and assorted other dangers that threaten us. Add to these the fear associated with the onset of a serious life-threatening illness and facing the reality of our own mortality. These and other threats to our peace and happiness give us plenty of reasons to be fearful, and courage is required in dealing with them.

As Christians, another great fear can come from the growing opposition to Christianity and the erosion of religious freedoms both here in our beloved country as well as abroad. In our passage, the apostle Paul instructs us to be a people of great courage and strength. The ideal for Christians, when it comes to courage, includes a quality of life based on our faith in the ever-present Spirit of Jesus

Christ. Here there is no "grin and bear it" helpless attitude, but a more natural and proactive one which can see opportunity in every challenge, and victory in every instance of opposition or persecution.

Courage is not only a duty for Christians, but also a constant possibility because we have placed our lives in the almighty hands of God. It makes itself evident through patient endurance, moral consistency, infectious optimism, and spiritual fidelity. *"If God is for us, who can be against us?"* (Romans 8:32 NIV).

"Be strong and courageous. Do not be terrified; do not be discouraged, for the Lord your God will be with you wherever you go" (Joshua 1:9 NIV).

Jun 16

Chuckle: *"I'd really like to die in my sleep like my grandfather. Not kicking and screaming like those others riding in the car with him."*

Quote: *"It is motive alone that gives character to the actions of men."* ~ Jean De La Bruyere

When Crises Come

"Then one of the synagogue rulers, named Jairus, came there. Seeing Jesus, he fell at his feet and pleaded earnestly with him, 'My little daughter is dying. Please come and put your hands on her so that she will be healed and live.' So Jesus went with him" (Mark 5:22-24 NIV).

As a pastor, my heart has often been deeply moved as I stood in the pulpit and looked out over a congregation, many of whom were suffering through severe crises in their lives. There's the wife of an abusive husband. There's the grieving family who recently lost a loved one. There's a husband and father who has just lost his job. There are the parents in extreme emotional pain because of a rebellious child. These are only a few examples of the pain and heartache that people suffer.

More than likely you have been the recipient of a ministry of kindness and love in your own life in a time of crisis. If so, you are keenly aware of the comfort you felt from just knowing someone cared. Knowing that someone loves you enough to share your burden or hurt gives added strength to see you through even the most difficult of times. Jairus' heart was broken at the plight of his beloved daughter, and because of his sorrow, he set aside his pride and threw himself at the feet of Jesus. He was desperate for help and recognized both his need and his helplessness.

If you are suffering through a crisis, the lesson for you here is that you must seek help if you are to make it through. Likewise, if you are aware of a crisis in someone else's life, Jesus would have you be sensitive to that need, as He was, and be willing to do whatever it takes to help that person endure the crisis and be strengthened by it. Because of His love and compassion, Jesus went with the man and restored life to his little girl who had died even as Jairus was searching for Jesus.

In Matthew 25, Jesus describes what our reaction should be to those in crises and need. We are to visit the sick, feed the hungry, clothe the naked, satisfy the thirsty, etc. Jesus saw such actions as indicative of our relationship with Him, and He had harsh words for those who choose to ignore the needs in people's lives around them. In our ministry to others, we are taught to imitate the love Jesus has shown toward us.

If you are in a crisis, first draw close to your Lord, then swallow your pride, and seek help. If you know someone in crisis, make the time to minister to that need in the name of Jesus as you would want someone to minister to you. It is a struggle for each of us, as Christians, to find the right words or action that will help alleviate the pain. But the important thing is for us to be willing to help. Then God will show us the best way to minister to a given need.

God will bless you as you bless others!

Jun 17

Chuckle: *"What'll you do when you are as big as your father?"*
"Diet," replied the young boy.
Quote: *"Have courage for the great sorrows of life and patience for the small ones; and when you have laboriously accomplished your daily task, go to sleep in peace. God is awake."*
~ Victor Hugo

Daily Dependence Upon God

"Arise, O LORD! Deliver me, O my God!" (Psalm 3:7a NIV). *"So be strong and take heart, all you who hope in the Lord!"* (Psalm 31:24 NIV).

Each of us can draw a valuable lesson from the experiences and words of King David. Verse 5 tells us David awoke from his peaceful sleep and asked God to guide his every move throughout the day, and rescue him from his enemies. David's enemies were the advancing armies of his rebellious son, Absalom, but we face our own enemies every day. Peter warns us, *"Be self-controlled and alert. Your enemy the devil prowls around like a roaring lion looking for someone to devour"* (1 Peter 5:8 NIV).

If we are to live the victorious life, we too must learn to call on the Lord for guidance and deliverance day by day. *"From the LORD comes deliverance"* (see Psalm 3:8a). We must learn to trust in Him for the victory each day that He alone can win for us. Every day we need God's power to help us defend ourselves from the wiles of Satan and the evil accomplices he has working for him.

This attitude of dependence on God is sometimes difficult for us because, after all, "I'm pretty good at taking care of myself." For this attitude of dependence to take root in our lives, we must humble ourselves to the point we realize that without God we can do nothing that really matters (see John 15:5b NIV).

A good habit that can help us stay dependent upon our Lord is the use of "breath prayers." This is a habit which takes time to develop, but the ultimate outcome should be a brief, one breath prayer before we make each daily decision facing us, whether minor or major. "Lord help me make the right decision in this matter."

Paul tells us to *"let this attitude be in you that is also in Christ Jesus"* (Philippians 2:5). It is God's desire to make us more like Jesus every day. If He is to do this, we must make ourselves pliable in His hands like clay is to the potter. As we depend upon Him for strength and allow ourselves to be molded into the likeness of Jesus, then our attitudes will become more and more like His.

Let's learn from David. Each morning when you awaken, take a moment to express your dependence on God and ask for His guidance and deliverance from evil influences during the day. Then follow this up during the day with breath prayers as you seek God's help in dealing with each issue you face. Ask God to give you the strength to walk in victory every moment of every day.

Chuckle: *"Two lawyers walked into the office one Monday morning, talking about their weekends. "I got a dog for my kids this weekend," said one.*

The other replied, "Good trade."

Quote: *"You may be only one person in the world, but you may also be the world to one person."* ~ Unknown Source

A Depraved Generation

"The human heart is most deceitful and desperately wicked. Who really knows how bad it is? But I know! I, the Lord, search all hearts and examine secret motives. I give all people their due rewards, according to what their actions deserve" (Jeremiah 17:9-10 NLT). *"Do everything without complaining or arguing, so that you may become blameless and pure children of God without fault in a crooked and depraved generation"* (Philippians 2:14-15 NIV).

The word "depraved" means totally wicked. It describes the condition of the human heart without the transforming work of the Holy Spirit through faith in the atoning blood sacrifice of Jesus Christ. When used in a Biblical sense, it implies that there is absolutely nothing we can do, in our own strength, to make ourselves less depraved.

Most of us would agree that we live among people of a depraved generation. When I read the paper or hear the news, I'm amazed and appalled by the utter wickedness within the human heart. We sometimes forget how evil the world really is.

Paul admonished the Christians at Philippi to be different and *"shine like stars in a universe"* (Philippians 2:15 NIV), while living in an otherwise evil generation of people. Paul's words remind me of the prayer of Jesus to His Father: *"My prayer is not that you take them (His followers) out of the world but that you protect them from the evil one . . . As you sent me into the world, I have sent them into the world"* (John 17:15-18 NIV).

God does not want us to blend in with the world. He wants us to stand out as different, even while we remain in the world as His messengers and ambassadors.

Jesus, in the Sermon on the Mount, says we are to be the salt of the earth and the light of the world to those around us. He goes on to say a light should be put on a stand so that its light can shine for all. *"In the same way, let your light shine before men that they may see your good deeds and praise your Father in heaven"* (Matthew 5:16 NIV).

When we blend in with the depraved crowd, we hide the light of Christ that has been entrusted to us. Here are some ways we hide our light:

- by being quiet when we should speak
- going along with the sinful ways of the crowd
- denying Jesus, the true Light
- letting sin dim our light
- not explaining our light to others
- ignoring the needs of others

Let's face it, a Christian has influence—either positive or negative. We must not hide from the world, but let our influence count for Christ in such a way that God will get the glory for all the good we do. We should be a beacon of truth and not allow our light of Christ be hidden from the rest of the world.

Jun 19

Chuckle: *Showing off his new hearing aids, Ralph said to his wife, "This is the world's best hearing aid. I haven't heard this well since I was a kid."*

"What kind is it?" asked his wife.

Glancing at his watch, Ralph said, "Oh, it's about two fifteen."

Quote: *"Never despair, but if you do, work on in despair."* ~ Edmund Burke

Giving Up in Despair

"We are hard pressed on every side by troubles, but we are not crushed and broken. We are perplexed, but don't (despair) give up and quit. We are hunted down, but God never abandons us. We are knocked down, but we get up again and keep going" (2 Corinthians 4:8-9 NLT).

To despair is to give up on life and lose all hope for the future. There's nothing quite as heart-breaking as seeing a Christian brother or sister so beaten down and discouraged by the cares of this world that they have lost all hope.

The apostle Paul suffered more terrible persecution, including physical pain, than you and I can imagine—all because of his love, faithfulness, and loyalty to his Lord. He was able to avoid despair and the temptation to give up because he received his strength and positive attitude from his dependence upon God's never ending presence and power in his life. He said, *"For I can do everything with the help of Christ who gives me the strength I need"* (Philippians 4:13 NLT).

It's easy for us to become discouraged and hopeless due to the crime and chaos we see every day in our world. Add to that other personal hardships which we confront in life and we have the formula for despair. But Jesus understood the troubles His followers would endure and said, *"Here on earth you will have many trials and sorrows. But take heart, because I have overcome the world"* (John 16:33b NLT).

When troubles and trials come, we should ask God for strength, work on, and don't despair.

During the Thirty Years' War in Europe (1618-1648), German pastor Paul Gerhardt and his family were forced to flee from their home. One night as they stayed in a small village inn, homeless and afraid, his wife broke down and cried openly in despair. To comfort her, Gerhardt reminded her of Scripture promises about God's provision and keeping. Then, going out to the garden to be alone, he too broke down and wept. He felt he had come to his darkest hour. Soon afterward, Gerhardt felt the burden lifted and sensed anew the Lord's presence. Taking his pen, he wrote a hymn that has brought comfort to many. "Give to the winds thy fears; hope, and be undismayed; God hears thy sighs and counts thy tears; God shall lift up thy head. Through waves and clouds and storms He gently clears the way. Wait thou His time, so shall the night soon end in joyous day."

It is often in our darkest times that God makes His presence known most clearly. He uses our sufferings and troubles to show us that He is our only source of strength. And when we see this truth, like Pastor Gerhardt, we receive new hope. Are you facing a great trial? Take heart. Put yourself in God's hands. Wait for His timing. He will give you a "song in the night.' ~ Our Daily Bread, May 7, 1992.

Chuckle: *What do you call 40 men watching the Super Bowl on TV? The Dallas Cowboys!"*

Quote: *"Love is not getting, but giving, not a wild dream of pleasure, and madness of desire . . .it is goodness, and honor, and peace and pure living."* ~ Henry van Dyke

Generosity Always Returns

"Give generously, for your gifts will return to you later. Divide your gifts among many, for you do not know what risks might lie ahead" (Ecclesiastes 11:1-2 NLT).

The disastrous earthquake in Haiti a few years back brought untold death and suffering to the Haitian people. The television images of corpses in the streets and helpless victims touched the hearts of people all over the world. People gave generously of their means, and many gave themselves by traveling to Haiti to help in any way they could. Some still do.

God's Word teaches us to be generous to the point of personal sacrifice when we see someone in need. I am both proud and thankful that Americans and others around the globe responded to the people of Haiti in such amazing ways.

I have heard it said that when you give something away, it will always come back to you in some form. This is a paradox that makes ultimate sense to a Christian. It is a principle that God planned for His children from the beginning. Give and it will be given to you. In the same way that a moisture laden cloud releases its rain, a Christian will be so full of God's grace that he or she will joyfully and generously release and share his or her blessings.

In our passage, Solomon summarizes that life involves both risk and opportunity. He seems to be saying that by giving to others, we are preparing for uncertain risks which may come later to us. This makes sense if we accept the premise that as we give, much will be given to us in return. We must grasp the opportunity to give when it comes while we have the ability and resources to do so. By doing so, we are showing a spirit of trust and adventure. We trust the goodness of God and the truths of His Word, and enjoy the adventure of seeing lives blessed by our generosity. As we give to others, we can be assured that blessings will return to us. God has a way of multiplying our generosity. As you give to help someone, that person will in turn help someone else, and the cycle continues.

I'm reminded of the words of Jesus: *"If you give, you will receive. Your gift will return to you in full measure, pressed down, shaken together to make room for more, and running over. Whatever measure you use in giving—large or small—it will be used to measure what is given back to you"* (Luke 6:38 NLT). As we treat others with generosity, graciousness, and compassion, these qualities will come back to us in full measure.

A well-known philanthropist was asked, "How is it that you give away so much, and yet have so much left?"

"I suppose it's like this," he replied. "I shovel out, and God shovels in, and he has a bigger shovel than I do!"

Chuckle: *Two boys were walking home from church after hearing a sermon on the devil. One asked the other, "What do you think about all this Satan stuff?"*

The other replied, "Well, you know how Santa Claus turned out. It's probably just your Dad."

Quote: *"The humblest citizen of all the land, when clad in the armor of a righteous cause, is stronger than all the hosts of error."* ~ William Jennings Bryan

The Whole Armor of God

"A final word: Be strong with the Lord's mighty power" (Ephesians 6:10 NLT).

Why do we find it so difficult to live the Christian life? Why are we beset by temptations that threaten to destroy us? Why do we have difficulty finding the words to be a witness for Christ? Why do our plans for Christian service often come to naught? What is wrong with us? The answer is rather simple—we have a powerful enemy whose goal it is to render us ineffective as representatives of Jesus Christ.

The good news is that God has provided us the protective spiritual armor to withstand Satan's attacks. Paul tells us to *"Put on all of God's armor so that you will be able to stand firm against the strategies and tricks of the Devil"* (Ephesians 6:11 NLT). As Christians we battle daily with the powerful evil forces of fallen angels headed by Satan. I'm sure you know from experience that he is vicious and relentless in his attacks. If we are to resist him, we need to avail ourselves of God's strength and utilize every piece of His armor.

Satan uses every enticement to lure us away from our Lord and to make us feel defeated and useless. He wants to neutralize us and make us of no value to Christ. He often uses evil people as his allies. However, the battle is best described as moral and spiritual warfare. Listen to a description of some of Satan's methods:

"These people are false apostles. They have fooled you by disguising themselves as apostles of Christ. But I am not surprised! Even Satan can disguise himself as an angel of light. So it is no wonder his servants can also do it by pretending to be godly ministers" (1 Corinthians 11:13-15a NLT).

We must depend upon the Holy Spirit for the ability to discern the truth and identify genuine Christians from those who are not.

How do we go about defending ourselves from being defeated by Satan's wiles? Paul lists several pieces of armor we need to put on. Briefly, these are salvation, truth, righteousness, peace, faith, God's Word, and prayer in the power of the Holy Spirit. I cannot adequately address each of these here, but I encourage you to study Ephesians 6 more fully.

The point Paul is making is that we need not be defeated, but victory does not come without adequate preparation and effort. His message is to the entire church, as well as to individual believers. Being active in the church—the Body of Christ—will provide you with the loving support of other Spirit-led Christians who will help you find the strength to resist the crafty and deceitful lures of the Evil One.

Jun 22

Chuckle: *"Do you believe in life after death?" the boss asked a new employee.*

"Yes, of course sir," the employee replied.

"Well then, that makes everything just fine," the boss went on. "After you left early yesterday to go to your grandmother's funeral, she stopped by to see you!"

Quote: *"His love enableth me to call every country my country, and every man my brother"* ~ Daniel Wheeler; "Spiritual Experiences of Friends."

Attitude of Love

"Do you think you deserve credit merely for loving those who love you? Even the sinners do that" (Luke 6:32 NLT).

Attitude is defined as: *"A way of acting or behaving that shows what one is thinking or feeling" (i.e. a loving attitude; a friendly attitude, etc).* The Scriptures tell us that God is Love. Since Jesus is God incarnate, He is love, and we are told *"Your attitude should be the same as that of Christ Jesus"* (Philippians 2:5 NIV). In other words, Christ would have us live every day with an attitude of love like His. What does such an attitude of love look like?

A Christian writer named Tertullian (160-225 AD) wrote these words: *"It is our care for the helpless, our practice of lovingkindness, that brands us in the eyes of many of our opponents. 'Look!' they say. 'How they love one another! Look how they are prepared to die for one another.'"* Tertullian describes an attitude of love among early Christians and emphasizes the positive impact this attitude will have on others, even those who oppose us.

Jesus set the example for us when it comes to loving people. He treated everyone with kindness and compassion. I'm sure He was aware that every person carries burdens and faces difficulties that influence the way they react. He knew they didn't need more problems and life challenges—they needed an extra measure of love

107

and understanding. Jesus said, *"Come to me, all you who are weary and burdened, and I will give you rest"* (Matthew 11:28 NIV). His love was unchanging and independent of how people reacted to Him. His attitude was one of unconditional love.

A belligerent, angry spirit against those who react with anger and hostility toward us does not reflect the attitude of love that Jesus modeled for us. The only effective tool we have to draw people to Christ and Christianity is the demonstrated unconditional love of Jesus Christ. Even though we cannot always understand why people react the way they do, we can still represent our Lord by being a blessing to them. Like the people described by Tertullian, they will certainly see Jesus in you if you have the attitude of love that Jesus has.

"Love of God is the root, love of our neighbor the fruit of the Tree of Life. Neither can exist without the other, but the one is cause and the other effect." ~ Illustrations for Biblical Preaching; Edited by Michael Green

Jun 23

Chuckle: *"If God had wanted me to touch my toes, he would have put them on my knees."*

Quote: *"Drop Thy still dews of quietness, Till all our strivings cease; Take from our souls the strain and stress, And let our ordered lives confess The beauty of Thy peace."* ~ John Greenleaf Whittier

Believing Brings Blessings

"You are blessed, because you believed that the Lord would do what he said" (Luke 1:45 NLT).

Great comfort and peace comes with the knowledge that a friend's word can be trusted without fear of deception or wavering from promises made. Isn't it wonderful to know a person is completely trustworthy and will do what he or she has promised— and will not do what he or she has promised not to do? Doesn't it give you a great sense of well-being when those around you can always be trusted to have your best interest at heart?

Living in an atmosphere of acceptance and trust reminds me of the relationship Jesus Christ wants with each of us as believers. He wants us to believe and trust Him even when His promises don't make sense to our finite minds. I've often heard that "taking God at His Word" is the essence of faith. Mary's great faith allowed her to believe and trust God when He promised she would be the mother of the long-awaited Messiah. She had no problem accepting the promise and assignment God had given her. Her faith and belief brought her great joy and peace. In the verses following our passage, Mary praises God for His grace, mercy, and promises kept.

God's Word is full of promises to His children. He promises to never leave or forsake us. He promises us eternal life, sealed by His Spirit, through faith in Jesus Christ. He promises that no power will ever separate us from His love. He promises that His Spirit will always live within us to give us strength, comfort, peace, instruction, and wisdom. These and many more promises of God should give us a great sense of joy and peace.

However, we often allow doubt to enter our minds, and we begin to see every problem and obstacle in our lives rather than opportunities to believe God. It's when we take our eyes off our Lord and begin to question His promises that our peace will be replaced with anxiety and fear.

If your life is filled with worry and anxiety, please take another look at God's promises and begin to trust Him fully in all circumstances. If you really believe and trust Him, you will experience a peace that surpasses human understanding. This deep and abiding peace will bring more blessings to your life than you have ever imagined.

Jun 24

Chuckle: *Question: "Who was the greatest comedian in the Bible?" Answer: "Samson. He brought the house down."*
Quote: *"Conviction of sin by the Holy Spirit blots out every relationship on earth and leaves one relationship only—'Against you, you only, I have sinned.'"* ~ Oswald Chambers

Challenge and Commitment

"Then I heard the voice of the Lord saying, 'Whom shall I send? And who will go for us?' Then I said, 'Here am I. Send me'" (Isaiah 6:8 NIV).

When Isaiah found himself in God's presence, he saw himself as wretchedly sinful and unworthy to behold God's holiness. He cried out in desperation, *"Woe to me for I am ruined! I am a man of unclean lips"* (Isaiah 6:5 NIV). His repentant cry of confession led God to forgive him of his sin and cleanse him. This process of confession, repentance, forgiveness, and cleansing had prepared Isaiah to hear the voice of God. God had prepared him and made him a suitable vessel which He could use.

Up to this point, God had been teaching Isaiah and creating an awareness in him that he could never accomplish anything of lasting value without God's presence and power. Jesus affirms this truth: *"I am the vine; you are the branches. If a man remains in me and I in him, he will bear much fruit; apart from me you can do nothing"* (John 15:5 NIV). Isaiah was now ready to hear God's call and challenge. He was now listening for that call because his heart had been made over into one that God could use.

I have had church members say, "I just don't hear God calling me to do this or that ministry." Without being judgmental, it could be that the reason one doesn't hear God's call is that he/she has not gone through the preparation process like Isaiah. When we have been cleansed, purified, and prepared, God will open our spiritual ears to His call.

Isaiah heard God's challenge: *"Whom shall I send?"* Because of the condition of Isaiah's heart, he never hesitated to accept the challenge, even before God had told him specifically what he wanted him to do. He was willing and committed no matter what the mission turned out to be. Like Isaiah, God cleanses and prepares us for service.

"Here am I. Send me," should always be our response in obedience to God's call. Millions have heard God's call down through the ages, and have responded with "Here am I. Send me!" As a result, multitudes have come to salvation in Christ. Isaiah was motivated to accept God's call because he "saw the Lord." Wherever you are, and regardless of your age or status in life, God wants you to see Him for who He is, hear Him, and accept the challenge He lays before you. God has no plan "B" for drawing people to Himself. We should be attuned to God's will and live to please Him.

Maybe you are sensing God's call on your life, but are not yet willing to respond with, "Here am I. Send me!" I pray God will give you the strength to do so, because true happiness and fulfillment as a Christian comes from knowing and doing His will.

Jun 25

Chuckle: *While walking on a beach, I heard someone shout, "Look, a dead bird!" I saw another person look up at the sky and say, "Where?"*

Quote: *"Live as if Christ died yesterday, rose this morning, and is coming back again tomorrow."* ~ Martin Luther

Commissioned for Service

"He, God, said, 'Go and tell this people'" (Isaiah 6:9 NIV).

After forgiving his sins, cleansing and purifying him, God called Isaiah to a mission. Isaiah said, *"Here am I. Send me!"* Now he was mentally and spiritually prepared to hear what God wanted him to do. This picture reminds me of how Jesus prepared His disciples to accept His commission by giving them to the greatest task ever assigned to anyone—*"Go and make disciples of all nations...."* (Matthew 28:19 NIV).

God commissioned Isaiah to prophesy to people whose hearts had become hardened beyond their ability to repent. This seems strange on the surface unless we understand that God had long range plans for His people and looked forward to the day when they would repent and return to Him.

Jesus confronted the same hardness of hearts as He preached here on earth. Not only did many not believe, but others were hostile toward Him. When God sends us, He knows the difficulties we will face. Nevertheless, He requires our faithfulness and has promised to always be with us. We can never use opposition or unbelief to justify our failure to share the message of Jesus Christ.

Sadly, many Christians never accept God's commission and never share Christ with anyone. Many experience guilt and shame for this, but seem powerless to change. Are you one who lacks the courage to share the gospel message of salvation through faith in Jesus Christ? Satan will try to convince you that you just aren't up to the task.

Here are some excuses I have heard and experienced: "I don't know enough Scripture;" "I'm afraid I will be rejected;" "I don't express myself well;" "I'm afraid of making a mistake, etc."

Each of these excuses features the personal pronoun "I." In other words, they show we are dependent upon our own strength and abilities to witness for Christ. We will always fail when we depend upon ourselves rather than God for courage, strength, and wisdom.

Now let's turn these excuses into positives: "God's Holy Spirit will help me share His Word;" "He will help me overcome the fear of rejection;" "He will give me the courage I need"; "He will give me the right words to say;" "He will take away my fear."

"At that time you will be given what to say, for it will not be you speaking, but the Spirit of your Father speaking through you" (Matthew 10:19b-20 NIV).

Depending upon our Lord means relying upon His promise, *"And surely I am with you always, to the very end of the age"* (Matthew 28:20 NIV). Your personal story about your faith and how Christ has changed your life is powerful when used by the Holy Spirit to draw others to Himself. Just relax and let our Lord guide you in your encounters with those who need Christ.

Above all, let others see Jesus in you by the way you live. Our Lord will never leave you nor fail you!

Jun 26

Chuckle: *"Wouldn't you know it . . . brain cells come and brain cells go, but fat cells live forever."*

Quote: *"Many receive advice, but the wise profit from it."*
~ Publilius Syrus

Advice and Instruction

"Get all the advice and instruction you can, and be wise the rest of your life" (Proverbs 19:20 NLT).

We all like to think we are wise and can make sensible decisions based on our own life experiences, education, and common sense. Teenagers can be resistant to advice, especially if it comes from mom and dad who, by definition, just don't know anything. But the problem is not limited to teenagers. Some of us older folks are so set in our ways that any advice that suggests changing the way we think and act is automatically rejected. We often rely on these overused words: "I've never done it that way." Today I challenge each of us to examine our attitudes toward receiving advice and counsel.

After watching the swing of a pupil, the golf pro began making suggestions for improvement. But each time the pupil interrupted with his own version of what was wrong and how to correct it. After a few minutes, the pro began nodding his head in agreement. At the end of the session, the student paid the pro, congratulated him on his expertise as a teacher, and left in an obviously pleased frame of mind.

An astonished observer asked the pro, "Why did you go along with him?"

"Son," the old pro said with a grin, as he pocketed his fee, "I learned long ago that it's a waste of time to try to sell answers to a man who only wants to buy echoes."

Obviously, not all advice is good advice. Larry Burkett put it this way: *"A wise man seeks much counsel . . . a fool listens to all of it."* We must learn to discern between wise and foolish counsel. But the point of this lesson is to open our minds to fresh and new ideas that can positively affect the way we live, make decisions, and relate to other people. Of course, our best sources of advice for living are God's Word and the counsel of godly people.

But we can close our spiritual ears to the point that we cannot accept advice even from God Himself. This attitude can prevail in an individual Christian or the entire church. A church can become so locked in tradition that form and format become more important than substance in worship. The Holy Spirit cannot work freely in such an environment.

A key ingredient of true wisdom is the recognition of the need for personal, intellectual, and spiritual counsel. This recognition should be combined with the willingness to accept and utilize advice and education, especially spiritual instruction. *"Fools think they need no advice, but the wise listen to others"* (Proverbs 12:15 NLT). The more we learn the more we realize how much we don't know. When our physical and spiritual minds are open to learning, we will become much more valuable in the Lord's work as we serve other people.

Chuckle: *"My teenage daughter thinks I'm too nosy. At least that's what she keeps writing in her diary."*

Quote: *"Of all the errors one could make, God's gospel plan is the wrong thing to be wrong about."* ~ Neal A. Maxwell

I'm Not Ashamed

"I am not ashamed of the gospel, because it is the power of God for the salvation of everyone who believes.." (Romans 1:16 NIV). Jesus said, *"If anyone is ashamed of me and my message, I, the Son of Man, will be ashamed of that person when I return to my glory and the glory of the Father and the holy angels"* (Luke 9:26 NLT).

Some time back I was pleasantly surprised to see ads running on television that showed several people of differing ages and ethnicities joyfully expressing their faith in Jesus Christ. The ad went something like this: "I'm not ashamed, I'm not ashamed, I'm not ashamed of the gospel of Jesus Christ." How refreshing it was to see such bold expressions of Christian faith by a group of ordinary people on national television. The ads I saw were aired on the FOX News Channel, but I have not seen them lately...

None of us should be ashamed of our faith because our message is the "good news" about Jesus Christ—a message of life-changing power and eternal salvation for everyone who believes. It is a matter of spiritual life or death. Sadly, too many of us do not express our faith boldly. Is this because we are ashamed of our Lord? Or is it because we tend to focus on our personal weaknesses and inadequacies, rather than the power of God's Spirit who will give us strength and embolden us? Many of us are like an Arctic River—frozen over at the mouth!

Boldly and lovingly expressing our faith is Jesus' plan for those who know Him as Savior and Lord. *"If anyone acknowledges me publicly here on earth, I will openly acknowledge that person before my Father in heaven. But if anyone denies me here on earth, I will deny*

Jerry Stratton

that person before my Father in heaven" (Matthew 10:32 NLT).

There's no way we can be faithful to carry out Christ's Great Commission unless we tell others about Jesus. Jesus said we are to *"go and make disciples of all nations (people), baptizing them in the name of the Father, and the Son, and the Holy Spirit. Teach the new disciples to obey all the commands I have given you. And be sure of this: I am with you always, even to the end of the age"* (Matthew 28:19-20 NLT).

Once, when walking down a Chicago street, D. L. Moody stepped up to a man, a stranger to him, and asked, "Sir, are you a Christian?"

"Mind your own business" was the reply.

Moody replied, "Sir, this is my business."

Chuckle: *A driver slowed when he saw the "sold out" sign. He pulled into the next station with $3.00 gas. He complained to the operator about the cheaper gas down the street, but they are sold out. The operator said, "Our gas is only $2.00 a gallon when we're sold out."*

Quote: *"There is a strength of quiet endurance as significant of courage as the most daring feats of prowess."*
~ Henry Theodore Tuckerman

Endurance Is Rewarded

"We must not become tired of doing good. We will receive our harvest of eternal life at the right time if we do not give up" (Galatians 6:9 NCV). *"So don't get tired of doing what is good. Don't get discouraged and give up, for we will reap a harvest of blessing at the appropriate time"* (Galatians 6:9 NLT).

Sometimes we come to places in life where just giving up and quitting seem to be the best alternatives. You may feel like you're banging your head against a wall in you work or profession. You may feel discouraged because of the choices made by your children or grandchildren. There will be many times in life when you will feel like throwing in the towel. Let's think together about what God would have us do in these situations.

First, let's keep in mind that our salvation is not earned by what we do—doing good is not enough. *"For it is by grace you have been saved, through faith—and this is not of ourselves, it is the gift of God—not by works, so that no one can boast"* (Ephesians 2:8-9 NIV).

If our salvation is not determined by our doing good works, what is the *"harvest of eternal life/blessing"* that Paul advances in our Galatians passage? I think the next verse in Ephesians 2 will help answer that question. *"For we are God's workmanship, created in Christ Jesus to do good works, which God prepared in advance for us to do"* (Ephesians 2:10 NIV).

If our salvation is by grace through faith, and God has

prepared the good works we are to do as Christians, what is our reward for faithfulness in fulfilling the purpose and good works God has planned? Listen to Paul again: *"If any man builds on this foundation (Jesus Christ) using gold, silver, costly stones, wood, hay or straw, his work will be shown for what it is, . . . It will be revealed with fire, and the fire will test the quality of each man's work. If what he has built survives, he will receive his reward. If it is burned up, he will suffer loss; he himself will be saved, but only as one escaping through the flames"* (1 Corinthians 3:12-15 NIV).

In summary, if you are born again Christian, your eternal life in heaven is assured. However, you should desire to please your Lord by living for Him through faithfully serving others—the good works God has planned for you to do. If you endure to the end by faithfully doing good, you will receive your rewards in heaven. Will you be one who receives a harvest of rewards or one who enters God's presence and receives no rewards?

Will you hear God say, *"Well done, good and faithful servant?"* (Matthew 25:21 NIV).

Jun 29

Chuckle: *"The good Lord didn't create anything without a purpose, but mosquitoes, armadillos, and sand gnats come close!"*
Quote: *"Church membership does not make you a Christian any more than owning a piano makes you a musician."*
~ Unknown Source

Where Is Your Devotion?

"Thomas said to him, My Lord and My God" (John 20:28 NIV).

What do you think brings the most pleasure to God? Is it what we do for Him, or our love relationship with Him? Do you try to please God by working for Him? Do you think that doing good deeds will somehow cause God to overlook your lack of devotion to Him? These probing questions deserve serious consideration.

I think many of us see God as our "sugar daddy," with the responsibility of meeting our every need. Granted, God can and will meet our every need, but should that be our focus? Jesus said the greatest commandment is to *"Love the Lord your God with all your heart and with all your soul and with all your mind and with all your strength"* (Mark 12:30 NIV).

When Jesus said, *"You will be my witnesses"* (Acts 1:8), He meant that we should live our lives with uncompromising love and devotion to Him and be determined to please Him wherever we are and in every circumstance. In John 15, Jesus asked Peter three times, *"Do you truly love me?"* It was only after Peter expressed his love for Him that Jesus told Peter to *"Feed my lambs."*

If there is anything in our lives that becomes more important to us than love for, and loyalty to, Christ, it's time for a spiritual check-up! It could be our love for our possessions or anything that causes us to take our eyes and devotion away from our Lord. One subtle competitor with our love, loyalty, and devotion to Christ is doing His work. We can become so busy doing the Kings work that we forget about the King.

Many measure themselves as Christians by how much they do—how many jobs they have in their church, etc. But the purpose of God's call on your life is for you to have a love relationship with Him, not a call to do something for Him. We are not sent to do things for God, but to be used of God, as He does His work through us—as His instruments by the power of the Holy Spirit—to further His agenda.

As our love for our Lord grows, we will be busy serving Him, but the motive for our service will be our love and devotion to Him. We won't just do "good things" in hopes of somehow gaining (earning) His approval. Our actions of service will have a single purpose, to bring honor and glory to God, not to ourselves.

Let's examine our hearts to determine if we are more dedicated to service than to the One we serve.

Jun 30

Chuckle: *A fella I hadn't seen in quite a while, said to me, "I thought you were dead!"*

"No," I said, "but I do have many of the symptoms."

Ponder this: *"We would often be ashamed of our best actions if the world only knew the motives behind them."*
~ Francois De La Rochefoucauld

Devotion to Christ

"I have been crucified with Christ and I no longer live, but Christ lives in me. The life I live in the body, I live by faith in the Son of God, who loved me and gave himself for me" (Galatians 2:20 NIV).

Have you given much thought to what it means to be fully devoted to Christ? In his Gettysburg Address, while dedicating the cemetery there, Abraham Lincoln used these words in reference to the soldiers buried there: "They gave the last full measure of devotion" to their country. This kind of devotion prompted soldiers to willingly give their lives for the object of that devotion. We do well to reflect on our own level of devotion to Jesus Christ.

Paul realized that Christ gave His last full measure of devotion when He died that we might live. He also recognized that to become like Christ should be the goal of every believer. In our passage, Paul says, in essence, that his old self had been crucified (died) so that Christ could become his life by living in him and through him. This is an awesome concept, and one that every Christian should aspire to live out. It means removing self so completely that our lives become Christ living in and through us.

Obviously, the first step in becoming completely devoted to Christ is to trust Him by faith as Savior. *". . . man is not justified by observing the law, but by faith in Jesus Christ"* (see verse 16). Saul (Paul) had previously worked hard to please God by observing and enforcing God's Old Testament laws—trying to live the "good" life. In his zeal to serve God, he became a chief persecutor of early

Christians. However, when he met Christ, he came to realize that living by a set of rules was inadequate, and that he could be reconciled to God only by faith in Jesus Christ. When he gave his heart and life to Christ, his old self died and now it is Christ living in him. When Christ died, our sins died with Him, and relationally we have become one with Christ. People will begin to see Christ in us.

It was Christ's love and sacrifice for him that motivated Paul in his devotion to Him. Because we have been crucified with Christ, we have been reconciled to God and are free to grow in Christ's likeness. In our daily lives, we have Christ's resurrection power as we continue to fight against sin. We are no longer alone because now Christ lives in us. He is our strength for living and our hope for the future.

What is your level of devotion to the Christ who gave His last full measure of devotion to us?

Jul 01

Chuckle: *A motorist, after being bogged down in a muddy road, paid a farmer twenty dollars to pull him out with his tractor. He said to the farmer, "At those prices, I should think you'd be pulling people out of the mud day and night."*

"Can't. At night I haul water for the hole."

Quote: *"The man who wins may have been counted out several times, but he didn't hear the referee."* ~ H. E. Jansen

Dealing with Failure and Defeat

"My days are over. My hopes have disappeared. My heart's desires are broken" (Job 17:11 NLT).

Let's learn together how to overcome failures and be victorious in our Christian living. In our passage, Job expresses how some of us feel at times. If you don't feel the need for a lesson on handling defeat and failure right now, just take note—you will at some point in your life.

John F. Kennedy once said, *"Success has many fathers, but failure is an orphan; no one wants to claim it."* Wouldn't it be wonderful if everything in life was successful—every relationship fulfilling? But even for Christians, life is a combination of both successes and failures, victories and defeats, gains and losses. And sadly, many of these failures we bring on ourselves by poor decisions and choices. But God has an answer for us.

First, we must realize that everyone fails. Peter failed his Lord miserably when he fled, along with the other disciples, from the Garden of Gethsemane (Matthew 26:56). And he failed again when he denied Jesus by saying he didn't know Him (Matthew 26:69-75). James 3:2 tells us, *"We all stumble in many ways."* Isn't that the truth? We all make mistakes— fumble the ball—mess up. It's not "if" but "when" we fail. We have to learn to deal with—and overcome— failure and defeat.

"There is not a righteous person on earth who does what is

right and never sins" (Ecclesiastes 7:20 NIV). No one is perfect. The very best basketball players only make 50% of their shots. The best baseball hitters only get one out of three. Babe Ruth hit 714 home runs, but struck out 1330 times. *"For all have sinned and fall short of God's glorious standard"* (Romans 3:23 NLT).

I heard about a preacher, who said to his congregation, *"let's bow our heads and pray for our falling shorts."*

R. P. Macy tried to start a department store seven times before he succeeded by founding the world famous Macy's of New York. Failure and defeat are as much a part of life as success and victory. But we have to learn to deal with and overcome them—and we have a source of strength to do just that.

God often gets your undivided attention after you have experienced failure. And He often takes you back to the time and place of your failure in order to teach you and create something wonderful in your life. He wants us to learn and profit from our failures.

Jul 02

Chuckle: *"What should you do when you see an endangered animal eating an endangered plant?"* ~ George Carlin

Quote: *"Jesus will not overlook your shortcomings or simply encourage you to do better the next time. He will give you victory in the midst of your failure."* ~ Henry Blackaby

Reasons for Failures

Simon answered, "Master, we've worked hard all night and haven't caught anything. But because you say so, I will let down the nets" (Luke 5:5 NIV).

Simon and the other fishermen had failed to catch fish after trying all night long. But when they obeyed Jesus and let down their nets where He directed, they caught so many fish that their nets were torn. As we think about ways we fail our Lord, ourselves, and each other, let's consider some reasons we do so.

First, we fail because we don't plan for victory. *"A sensible man watches for problems ahead and prepares to meet them. The simple minded man never looks (ahead) and suffers the consequences"* (Proverbs 27:12 TLB). To fail to plan is to plan to fail. When we don't see the future with God's vision and direction, we fail. Success comes when God's plans become our own.

Second, we fail because we give up too soon. *"Let us not become weary in doing good, for at the proper time we will reap a harvest if we do not give up"* (Galatians 6:9 NIV). We may want to throw in the towel and say, "I just can't study the Bible and pray every day—I just can't be a witness for Christ."

The path of least resistance usually leads to failure. Thomas Edison tried 200 different ways to make an incandescent light bulb before succeeding. He had learned 200 ways that didn't work and one way that did.

We learn through our failures if we will let God teach us. If we reject God and go our own way to failure, the lessons learned are often painful. I'm still learning, but God says, "Don't give up—don't quit—keep at it." The neat thing about a postage stamp is that it sticks to one thing all the way to its destination. God does the same for us.

Third, we fail because we're afraid to take risks. *"Fearing people is a dangerous trap, but to trust the Lord means safety"* (Proverbs 29:25 NIV). We're often afraid to take risks. "Lord, I hate my job, but I need the money—I can't risk changing." But God says, "Here's what I want you do and I'll be with you."

"I can do all things through Christ who gives me strength" (Philippians 4:13: NIV). The greatest failure is not trying.

Fourth, we fail because we go our way rather than God's way. *"There is a way that seems right to a man, but in the end it leads to death"* (Proverbs 14:12 NIV). By our actions, we say our ways are better than what God wants for us. It's my selfish, egotistical, stubborn way that leads to failure, defeat, and disappointment. *"We all, like sheep, have gone astray; each of us has turned to his own way"* (Isaiah 53:6 NIV). God's way always leads to success. *"My ways are not your ways; my thoughts are not your thoughts"* (Isaiah 55:8 NIV).

If you are enduring defeat and failure, God wants to give you victory and will do so if you turn to Him and His Word for answers.

Jul 03

Bumper Snicker: *"I've taken a vow of poverty. To annoy me, send money."*

Quote: *"If you have recently experienced failure, you may be on the brink of receiving a profound revelation from God!"*
~ Henry Blackaby

Failures Need Not Be Permanent

"People who cover over their sins will not prosper. But if they confess and forsake them, they will receive mercy" (Proverbs 28:13 NLT).

If we are serious about overcoming defeat and failure, we must do two things:

First, we must accept responsibility for our failures. We are greatly blessed to serve a God who specializes in second chances. Where would any of us be if it were not so? Can you honestly say, "I've never needed a second chance?" I doubt it.

Losers blame others, but those who learn to deal with defeat/failure say, "I have sinned/failed—it's my fault —I want to start over. I want God to do something special in my life." We can say to our family, our friends, our church family, "I'm the one who failed. I take responsibility. I need to admit it."

In 1977, after 88 straight wins, the UCLA Bruins lost a basketball game to Notre Dame. The next day, the LA papers had this headline, "blame me, says the coach!." He said, "I let my team get over-confident."

Until you say, "I am a sinner—I'm at fault—I need a Savior," you can never be saved and become a Christian. As Christians, we can never experience the real success God wants for us until we recognize our failures and sins, and ask forgiveness. *"For though a righteous man falls seven times, he rises again"* (Proverbs 24:16 NIV).

God reaches down His hand in the midst of life's failures, our sins, and our defeats to lift us up. He restores our joy and fellowship with Him.

"The Word of the Lord came to Jonah a second time" (Jonah, 3:1 NIV). Jonah failed miserably the first time God called him to a mission in Nineveh. But after his repentance, God gave him a second chance. Today, He's saying to you and to me, "no matter how many failures you've experienced, or the severity of those failures, I will give you another chance." Maybe you're wallowing in self-pity—or caught up in pride or stubbornness. God wants you to admit your failure and let Him help you start again.

Second, we must accept God's grace and forgiveness. *"If anyone is in Christ, he is a new creation; the old has gone; the new has come"* (2 Corinthians 5:17 NIV). No matter what has happened in your life, God will give you a new and transformed life through faith in Jesus Christ. He took our sins upon Himself on the cross.

I want to challenge you to love our Lord with all your heart and love your brothers and sisters as Jesus has loved us. *"Love never fails."* There is only one failure we need to fear. *"My grace is sufficient for you, my power is made perfect in weakness"* (2 Corinthians 12-9 NIV). His grace prevents eternal failure through faith in Jesus Christ.

For Christians, His grace is sufficient to pick you up in the midst of your failure and give you a new start. He will restore your joy and peace if you turn to Him in repentance.

Jul 04

Chuckle*: "A little boy told his pastor he was giving up something: His Mom was giving up candy; his Father ice cream, and he was giving up squash!"*

Quote: *"When you find yourself in a hole, stop digging!"*
~ Will Rogers

Life in the Pits

"I waited patiently for the Lord; he turned to me and heard my cry. He lifted me out of the slimy pit, out of the mud and mire; he set my feet on a rock and gave me a firm place to stand. He put a new song in my mouth, a hymn of praise to our God" (Psalm 40:1-3 NIV).

Erma Bombeck once said, *"If life is a bowl of cherries, how come I'm always in the pits?"* A good question!

Are there times when you feel everything is going wrong? Do you feel depressed at times with the hand you have been dealt in life? Are you discouraged because of physical limitations? Are your circumstances causing an attitude of despair? If so, you have a lot of company. Many feel, or have felt, this way.

There are two basic kinds of pits: those that come upon us, and those we dig for ourselves. We do well to examine the reasons we are in the pits. We are all subject to such feelings from time to time, but for Christians, there is a solution—God can deliver you. From Psalm 40, the psalmist David shares with us how God lifted him out of a terrible situation in his life. What can we learn from our passage?

When we find ourselves in the pits, wait on God in an attitude of faith and expectancy. Notice how David waited patiently on the Lord to help him in his time of need. The Hebrew word for "waited" means to wait with hope and expectation. This is a picture of "tip-toe" expectation, not "finger-tapping" impatience. We are an impatient people who want everything right now, if not sooner! We might be praying something like this: "Lord, give me patience and give it to me right now!"

God always has a purpose for making us wait for His timing. He wants us to exchange our strength for His. *"But those who wait on the Lord will find new strength. They will fly on wings like eagles; they will run and not grow weary, they will walk and not faint"* (Isaiah 40:31 NLT). While David waited, God was strengthening and shaping and him for future service.

Waiting for God to help us is not easy, but David received at least four clear benefits from waiting. God changed his attitude and lifted him out of his despair, gave him a sense of security by setting his feet on solid ground, gave him new strength and steadied him as he walked, filled his heart with joy, and put a new song of praise in his mouth.

There is no better place than the pits for God to get our attention, test our patience, and force us to wait upon Him with optimistic expectations.

Jul 05

Chuckle: *On his first safari, the American visitor sidled up to the experienced native guide and said smugly, "I know that carrying a torch will keep the lions away."*

"That's true," the guide replied, "but it depends on how fast you carry the torch."

Quote: *"O Lord our God, grant us grace to desire thee with our whole heart; that so desiring, we may seek, and seeking, find thee; and so finding thee, may love thee; and loving thee, may hate those sins from which thou hast redeemed us."* ~ St. Anselm

Delight in the Lord

"Delight yourself in the Lord and he will give you the desires of your heart" (Psalm 37:4 NIV).

Do you and I really know and understand the deepest desires of our hearts? I think many of us deal mostly with the superficial wants in our lives, but do not take the time to let God show us how to touch the innermost and most important desire of our hearts. We may think we know what we want and go about trying to get it while our deepest yearning goes unsatisfied—the desire that pleases God most. Yes, it is God's desire that you delight in Him—that you find your ultimate joy and pleasure in Him.

As God created us, He designed and shaped us to desire and delight in Him above all else. The psalmist put that desire this way, *"As the deer pants for streams of water, so my soul pants for you, O God"* (Psalm 42:1 NIV). God made our hearts for Himself because He understands that we will only be truly happy and content when He becomes our greatest delight. As we take delight in our Lord, we will commit our life to Him, and everything we do will be to glorify Him.

How do we go about making God our greatest desire and delight? Well, let's think about it from a human relationship point of view. When we delight in someone, it's usually someone we know well and we experience great pleasure and extreme joy while in his or her presence. Similarly, if we are to delight in the Lord, we must draw closer to Him and constantly seek to know Him better by spending time with Him. Our delight is also heightened when we stop to consider how much He loves us.

If lasting happiness and contentment could be found in having material things, then most of us should be deliriously happy and content beyond description. But the things of this world can never bring us the contentment and fulfillment for which our God-made hearts so desperately yearn. Without God there will always be a great unfilled void in our lives. But if we continue to seek our happiness in the Lord, He will provide what our hearts desire most— peace and contentment. If we delight in the Lord and seek Him as our most treasured possession, He will give us our greatest desire which, in reality, is Himself.

"Rejoice in the Lord always, I will say it again; Rejoice!" (Philippians 4:4 NIV).

Jul 06

Chuckle: *"College: a four-year period when parents have access to the phone."*

Quote: *"O most merciful Redeemer, Friend and Brother, May we know Thee more clearly, Love Thee more dearly, Follow Thee more nearly: For ever and ever."* ~ Sir Richard of Chichester

Equipped for Service

Jesus said, "Peace be with you! As the Father has sent me, I am sending you." And with that he breathed on them and said, "Receive the Holy Spirit" (John 20:21-22 NIV).

No doubt you have felt inadequate for the tasks our Lord has given us (e.g. Matthew 28:19-20). These feelings are directly from Satan who wants you to "throw in the towel" and give up. However, if we truly have the desire to be obedient to our Lord, we will search the Scriptures prayerfully, in the power of the Spirit, to find the strength to make obedience not only possible, but the source of unspeakable peace and joy.

Our passage records Jesus' appearance to His disciples after His resurrection. Once again, Jesus identified Himself with the Father, who provided the authority for everything He had done. Then an amazing and powerful commissioning ceremony occurs. With three simple—yet amazing—statements, Jesus equips the disciples (us) with everything they (we) would ever need to carry out the mission given them (and us).

First, Jesus gave them His peace. *"Peace be with you!"* Here Jesus reiterated a promise He had made previously, just prior to His crucifixion. *"Peace I leave with you; my peace I give you ... do not be afraid"* (John 14:27 NIV). Paul describes this peace as a supernatural peace *"which transcends all understanding and will guard your hearts and minds in Christ Jesus"* (Philippians 4:7 NIV). With this kind of peace, all fear, doubt, and uncertainty are removed.

Second, Jesus gave them His purpose. *"As the Father has sent me, I am sending you."* Jesus affirms that their authority in carrying out the mission given them comes directly from Him. Jesus demonstrated how they (we) are to go about sharing the good news of Jesus Christ with a lost world. He has told us what to do and showed us how to do it with love, mercy, and compassion.

Third, Jesus gave them His power. . . He breathed on them and said, *"Receive the Holy Spirit."* Here Jesus gave His closest disciples an early gift of the same Holy Spirit that was made available to all Christians on the day of Pentecost. *"And they were all filled with the Holy Spirit and spoke the word of God boldly"* (Acts 4:31 NIV). The guidance and power of the Holy Spirit are necessities in everything we try to do for our Lord. When we try to do God's work in our own strength, we will fail at every turn. Jesus said, *"If a man (person) remains in me and I in him, he will bear much fruit; apart from me (my Spirit) you can do nothing"* (John 15:5 NIV).

Do you have His peace? Have you accepted His purpose as your own? Have you accessed the power if the Holy Spirit to make it all possible? I pray you have.

Jul 07

Chuckle: *A man walked into a bank to hold it up and gave the teller a note that read, "This is a stickup. Give me all your money." She passed a note back to him that said, "Fix your tie. We're taking your picture."*

Quote: *"Humility is a voluntary abdication of power, wherever one's own advantage and one's self-assertion is involved."*
~ Ladislaus Boros

He Must Become Greater

"He (Jesus) must become greater and greater, and I must become less and less" (John 3:30 NLT).

It seems to be human nature to want to elevate our importance in the eyes of others. Pride causes us to want to take credit for the good in our lives and to blame others for the negative. The words of our passage were spoken by John the Baptist in describing his role in God's kingdom as compared to that of Jesus. He would never allow himself to be placed on a pedestal equal to or above that of His Lord. John had been sent by God to herald the coming of the Messiah.

Every day, as Christians, we are tempted to claim honor for ourselves for things obviously accomplished by God's power or the efforts of others. John's eagerness to subordinate himself and decrease his own importance reflects unusual humility. Pastors, teachers, deacons, and other Christian leaders are often tempted to call attention to their own success rather than Christ, the One they supposedly serve.

Humility becomes especially difficult when others heap praise upon us for our ministry and service. Allowing pride to replace humility has caused the downfall of some otherwise great Christian leaders. But making ourselves less that Christ may become greater is something each of us must deal with every day. Problems in this area are not limited to the more prominent Christians.

Corrie Ten Boom was once asked if it was difficult for her to remain humble. Her reply was simple, "When Jesus rode into Jerusalem on Palm Sunday on the back of a donkey, and everyone was waving palm branches and throwing garments on the road, and singing praises, do you think that for one moment it ever entered the head of that donkey that any of that was for him?" She continued, "If I can be the donkey on which Jesus Christ rides in His glory, I give him all the praise and all the honor."

The principle of making ourselves less is also applicable in our dealing with other people, as well as with our Lord. When we give credit to others and refuse credit ourselves, we are reflecting the attitude of Jesus when He said He came not to be served but to serve. *"Your attitude should be the same as that of Christ Jesus"* (Philippians 2:5 NIV).

When we give credit to God and to others rather than ourselves, we will be elevated in their eyes much more than if we try to draw attention to ourselves. Jesus said to His followers, *". . . whoever wants to be great among you must be your servant, and whoever wants to be first must be your slave"* (Matthew 20:26-27 NIV).

Chuckle: *What is an eyedropper (i-drop-ur)? A clumsy ophthalmologist.*

Quote: *"Man still wishes to be happy even when he so lives as to make happiness impossible."* ~ St Augustine of Hippo

Why Not Be Happy?

"So I concluded that there is nothing better for people than to be happy and to enjoy themselves as long as they can. And people should eat and drink and enjoy the fruits of their labor, for these are gifts from God" (Ecclesiastes 3:12-13 NLT).

God wants His people to be happy and optimistic about today and about the future. I don't think it pleases our Lord when we are grouchy, grumpy, and pessimistic Christians. It's sometimes easier, however, for us to dwell on the things that are wrong and unpleasant in our lives than to focus on all the blessings that God gives us every day. As I read this passage, I'm reminded of another one: *"Every good and perfect gift is from above, coming down from the Father of the heavenly lights, who does not change like shifting shadows"* (James 1:17 NIV).

I think we often look for happiness in the wrong places. It's tempting for us to look at the years gone by as times of true happiness. We may say something like, "Oh, how I wish I could go back to those good old days!" We can fail to see all the reasons we should be happy today instead of dwelling on the past. God wants us to enjoy life and be happy in our relationship with Him today and every day, even in the face of physical limitations, pain, heartache, financial difficulties, etc.

You may say, "But Jerry, you don't understand. With all my problems, I just don't have much to be happy about." I understand the feeling. However, I'm also convinced that we sometimes let such feelings overtake us without taking inventory of the happiness-producing blessings available to us—our children, grandchildren, other family members, friends, fellow believers, and most of all—a God that loves us with a love that exceeds our ability to fully understand.

True happiness is a matter of choice. When we chose to look to God for happiness rather than the past or our current circumstances, we are often amazed at how our attitude toward life changes. We find ourselves being happy in spite of the difficulties and challenges we face. With the proper view of God, we will find happiness as we enjoy all the good gifts He showers on us.

What is it in your life that really makes you happy?

"Happy the man (person) to whom 'tis given
To eat the bread of life in heaven;
This happiness in Christ we prove,
Who feed on His forgiving love."
~ Charles Wesley Hymn

Jul 09

Chuckle: *"The only people who listen to both sides of a family quarrel are the next-door neighbors."*

Quote: *"Character cannot be developed in ease and quiet. Only through experience of trial and suffering can the soul be strengthened, vision cleared, ambition inspired, and success achieved."*
~ Helen Keller

Hard Times: Why Do They Come?

"Now I want you to know, brothers, that what has happened to me has really served to advance the gospel. As a result, it has become clear throughout the palace guard and to everyone else that I am in chains for Christ. Because of my chains, most of the brothers in the Lord have been encouraged to speak the word of God more courageously and fearlessly" (Philippians 1:12-14 NIV).

Paul is in prison in Rome. While there he learned—and teaches us—that God can use even our most adverse circumstances for His glory. He can use the hard times in our lives to grow us spiritually and to accomplish His purposes.

God's people should prepare for hard times. *"Now I want you to know brothers . . . what has happened to me."* Good people will have bad experiences while living in this fallen world. Our Lord told His disciples, *"In this world you will have trouble. But take heart! I have overcome the world"* (John 16:33 NIV). Peter said, *"Dear friends, do not be surprised at the painful trial you are suffering, as though something strange were happening to you"* (1 Peter 4:12 NIV).

Paul was a classic example of this truth—he suffered much. He said, *"I have worked harder, been in prison more frequently, been flogged more severely, and have been exposed to death again and again . . ."* (2 Corinthians 11:23-28 NIV). *"For it has been granted to you on behalf of Christ not only to believe on Him, but also to suffer for Him"* (Philippians 1:29 NIV).

God's people should keep hard times in perspective. *". . . what has happened to me has really served to advance the gospel,"* (vs.12). Notice that Paul did not direct attention to himself and his suffering, but focused on the good that came from his hard times. There's a big difference between suffering to draw attention to ourselves and suffering for the Savior. We must be careful which we do.

When we suffer, the emphasis should not be on how much we suffer, but on what God was able to accomplish through it—how He used our struggles to accomplish His perfect work. Paul told Timothy, *"This is my gospel, for which I suffer even to the point of being chained like a criminal. But God's Word is not chained"* (2 Timothy 2:8-9 NIV). Our struggles can become vehicles by which we bring glory and honor to Him.

"The trials of our faith are like God's ironing. When the heat of trials is applied to our lives the wrinkles of spiritual immaturity begin to be smoothed out." ~ Unknown Source

Jul 10

Chuckle: *"The toughest part of a diet isn't watching what you eat. It's watching what other people eat."*

Quote: *"I think that if ever a mortal heard the voice of God it would be in a garden at the cool of the day."* ~ F. Frankfort Moore

Listening for God's Voice

"When he has brought out all his own, he goes ahead of them, and his sheep follow him because they know his voice" (John 10:4 NIV).

Many people have a problem with the concept of hearing the voice of God. One can be branded as strange if he claims to have heard God's voice. I heard a pastor present a wonderful message on this subject. I will share some of his thoughts, as well as my own, to hopefully shed some light on the subject.

First, it is possible to hear God's voice. In our first passage, Jesus uses the analogy of a shepherd and his sheep to make a point about our relationship to Him, the Good Shepherd. His sheep know Him and they recognize His voice. *"My sheep listen to my voice; I know them, and they follow me"* (vs. 27). Some lyrics from the old hymn, "In The Garden," come to mind. *". . . and he walks with me and he talks with me, and he tells me I am his own. And the voice I hear falling on my ear none other has ever known."* Yes, it is possible to hear God's voice, and He speaks to us in various ways: His Word, prayer, life's circumstances, and other people.

Second, it is normal to hear God's voice. Jesus refers to His followers as friends, *"I no longer call you servants, because a servant does not know his master's business. Instead, I have called you friends, for everything I have learned from my Father I have made known to you"*(John 15:15 NIV). What is more normal than a conversation with friends and family—to let them hear your voice? John 1:12 tells us that, as believers, we are the "children of God," and Ephesians 2:19 tells us we are "members of God's household." In the Old Testament there are many references to God's people listening for and hearing

His voice. It is a normal part of our relationship with God to hear Him.

Third, it is expected that we hear God's voice. *"If only you listen obediently to the voice of the LORD your God, . . ."* (Deuteronomy 15:5). *"Here I am! I stand at the door and knock. If anyone hears my voice and opens the door, I will come in and eat with him, and he with me"* (Revelation 3:20 NIV). God wants and expects us to listen intently for His voice, but often we are not listening because our hearts are turned away from Him—perhaps because we fear He may ask us to do something we don't want to do. Or He might say something we don't want to hear. Then God could be screaming at us, but we don't hear. *"But if thine heart turn away, so that thou wilt not hear, but shall be drawn away to worship other gods and serve them . . ."* (Deuteronomy 30:17 KJV).

If we want to hear God's voice, we must listen intently. We should always be leaning forward toward God in anticipation, while "cupping" our spiritual ears, so to speak, for fear that we might miss something God wants to say to us.

Jul 11

Chuckle: A *preacher asked for a discount at a store saying,* "You know I'm a poor preacher."

"*I know," said the storekeeper. "I heard you last night!*"

Quote: "*It was a Person that God gave, it is a Person that we need, and it is a Person that we accept by faith.*"
~ Walter Lewis Wilson

Believing God

"*. . . whatever you ask for in prayer, believe (have faith) that you have received it and it will be yours*" (Mark 11:24 NIV). "*If any of you lacks wisdom, he should ask God, . . . But when he asks, he must believe and not doubt*" (James 1:6 NIV).

Think back with me to yesterday—from the time you awoke until you went to bed last night. How many times did you face issues in your life that made you feel inadequate and lacking in the wisdom needed to deal with the situation(s) you were facing? If, after reflecting on this question, you answer "none," then you probably went through the day depending entirely upon your own strength and wisdom to make decisions and deal with issues you faced. You see, even if we think we know the best answer to a problem, or the best way to handle a situation, we may be settling for second best wisdom—ours.

From our two passages above, we see that believing—having faith—is essential for God to answer our prayers and grant our requests. Faith is believing God and acting on that belief. "If God says it, I believe it, and I will ask Him about it!" When you pray, do you do so with expectation and confidence that God will answer? Or is prayer just one more possibility among other sources you depend upon for wisdom and strength in your daily life? Maybe you pray something like this: "OK, Lord, I'm asking, but I don't really believe you will answer my prayer." What kind of faith is that???

A doubting Christian is one who says he trusts God, but really doesn't. He says he has faith, but he really doesn't. He is divided inside. God says he is "double-minded." *"That person should not think he will receive anything from the Lord; he is a double-minded person, unstable in all he does"* (James 1:7-8 NIV).

A double-minded Christian is one who knows Christ as Savior and is going to heaven, but on a daily basis does not have the faith to trust God to grant his or her request for wisdom to guide his or her life. We can pray all night to no avail unless we believe and have faith. As we mature in our Christian life, our faith should grow as well. What is it in your life that holds you back from believing God and exercising your faith in Him?

"At a circus a huge elephant was tied to an eighteen-inch stake. Could he not easily have pulled it out of the ground and been free? Sure! But he had tried it when he was a baby and was unsuccessful. The elephant had concluded that he could never pull it out of the ground. So there he stood, a massive creature capable of lifting whole trees, yet held captive by a puny stake. What small stake could faith release you from?"

Jul 12

Chuckle: *A child was asked to complete this statement: Laugh and the world laughs with you. Cry and . . . . "someone yells, 'Shut up!'"*

Quote: *"Finding God is not our greatest need; rather it is recognizing Him in each of life's ever-present situations, and then submitting to His will." ~* William Ward

Confessing Jesus as Lord

". . . in human form he obediently humbled himself even further by dying a criminal's death on a cross. Because of this, God raised him up to the heights of heaven and gave him a name that is above every other name. So that at the name of Jesus every knee will bow, in heaven and on earth and under the earth, and every tongue will confess that Jesus Christ is Lord, to the glory of God the Father" (Philippians 2:8-11 NLT).

As I contemplated this passage, I was reminded of a TV commercial where an automobile repairman says, "pay me now or pay me later." He says we can pay him to fix a minor problem at little cost, or we can wait until the problem becomes more serious and costs much more to repair.

We can confess Jesus as our Lord and Savior now while we still have time and it only costs us our faith and trust in Him. Or we can wait until the last judgment, when it will be too late to save us and the cost will be spending eternity separated from God in a place the Bible calls "hell." Not a pleasant thought.

This is one of the most profound passages in Scripture. At the last judgment—if not before—every human being will bow down and confess that Jesus Christ is Lord. It describes the exalted position of Jesus and the power of His name, which is far greater than any other. *"Salvation is found in no one else, for there is no other name under heaven given to men by which we must be saved"* (Acts 4:12 NIV).

For those of us who know Christ as Savior and Lord, this passage affirms our faith and the joy we experience from having confessed who He is, repented of our sins, received His forgiveness, and asked Him into our lives. Our confession of Jesus includes thanksgiving, praise, and life-long commitment to Him. My prayer is that you have made such a commitment to the King of Kings and Lord of Lords.

"A man was shown a red glass bottle and asked what he thought was in the bottle. He replied, 'wine? brandy? whiskey?' When told it was full of milk, he could not believe it until he saw the milk poured out. He hadn't known that the bottle was made of red glass which hid the color of the milk. So it was with our Lord's humanity. Men saw him tired, hungry, suffering, weeping, and thought he was only a man. He was made in the likeness of men, yet he ever is God over all, blessed forever." ~ Illustrations for Biblical Preaching; Edited by Michael P. Green

Jul 13

Chuckle: *"We never really grow up, we only learn how to act in public."*

Quote: *"Man must evolve for all human conflict a method which rejects revenge, aggression and retaliation. The foundation of such a method is love."* ~ Martin Luther King, Jr.

Dealing with Conflict

"Love must be sincere. . . Love each other as brothers and sisters and honor others more than you do yourself" (Romans 12:9,10 CEV). *"Starting a quarrel is like breaching a dam; so drop the matter before a dispute breaks out"* (Proverbs 17:14 NIV).

Are you involved in a conflict situation with a brother or sister? Is there someone who really gets under your skin by their words or actions, and causes you to rise up in defiance with a desire to retaliate? Conflict does not have to be all out war to have devastating effects on our overall demeanor and our fellowship with fellow believers—not to mention destroying our joy and fellowship with our Lord. Unresolved mild differences can escalate into much more serious disputes when we allow ourselves to become angry and bitter.

Perhaps you are reluctant to try reconciliation because you don't know how he/she will react to your overtures. But it really doesn't matter how they might react—you still have the responsibility to love them and honor them above yourself. You may say, "but God must not understand what He is asking me to do. He must not understand how I feel and the fears and anxieties I'm experiencing." Oh, yes He does.

God wants to teach us about Christ-like love, the kind of love that allowed Jesus to pray from the cross on behalf of those who were crucifying Him: *"Father, forgive them for they do not know what they are doing"* (Luke 23:34 NIV). Jesus said, *"My command is this: Love each other as I have loved you"* (John 15:12 NIV). We must trust the Holy Spirit to help us show love to those for whom we may not feel love. We cannot do it in our own strength.

We can honor and show love to those with whom we have conflict by trying to understand their points of view. By viewing the issue from their perspective, you will be better able to display a Christ-like spirit toward them. Try to see them through the eyes of Jesus—as His precious children for whom He died. Pray for them, give them the benefit of the doubt, and be willing to forgive.

Love and forgiveness are keys to resolving conflicts. *"Bear with each other and forgive whatever grievances you may have against another. Forgive as the Lord forgave you"* (Colossians 3:13 NIV).

Jul 14

Chuckle: Child's comment on the Bible: *"Moses died before he ever reached Canada. Then Joshua led the Hebrews in the battle of Geritol."*

Quote: *"It takes two to make a quarrel, but only one to end it."* ~ Spanish Proverb

Conflict Between Christians

"And now I want to plead with those two women, Euodia and Syntyche. Please, because you belong to the Lord, settle your disagreement. And I ask you, my true teammate, to help these women, for they worked hard with me in telling others the Good News. And they worked with Clement and the rest of my co-workers, whose names are written in the Book of Life" (Philippians 4:2-3 NLT).

Paul addressed the conflict between two prominent women in the church at Philippi, but conflict among Christians is no respecter of gender. It can happen to anyone, especially if our hearts aren't constantly focused on Jesus Christ, and on keeping the main thing the main thing—the Great Commandment and the Great Commission found in Matthew 22:37-38, 28:19-20.

Conflict between these two influential church leaders was no small matter because many had become believers through their efforts. Their credibility, and the credibility of Christianity, was on trial before these new and impressionable believers. Conflict within a congregation can drive people away and destroy the church's witness. If conflict exists in your church, this passage contains an important message for you. If not, there is a helpful preventive message as well. Let's glean some truths from these words.

First, in love we should always find a way to reconcile our differences. Paul pleaded with the women to take the initiative in reconciliation—to take responsibility for restoring their relationship and fellowship. Jesus said we are to take the initiative by going to the person who has something against us and reconcile our differences (see Matthew 5:23).

Please don't ignore festering anger, resentment, and hurt, no matter who is at fault. It will only get worse, and will control your life and rob you of joy and peace. Paul also asked them to seek to be like-minded with Christ. *"Let this mind be in you, which was also in Christ Jesus"* (Philippians 2:5 KJV). Differences should not result in irresolvable conflict. Differences should be addressed in an atmosphere of love, understanding, and concern for the feelings of the other person. Ask, 'What would Jesus do?'

Second, sometimes even the most mature Christians need help to overcome their differences, especially if they cannot, or will not, work out their problems themselves. Notice that Paul asked an unidentified loyal ministry teammate to act as a peacemaker and encourage reconciliation between the women. Jesus said, *"Blessed are the peacemakers, for they will be called the children of God"* (Matthew 5:9 NIV). Wise peacemakers give those on both sides of the conflict a way out without placing blame.

Differences can usually be worked out if the parties seek to see the other through the eyes of Christ—as a beloved human being for whom Christ willingly gave Himself.

Jul 15

Chuckle: *"Billy Graham once said that heaven would be like a big family reunion that never ends. Makes you shudder to think what hell must be like!"*

Quote: *"There are two ways to study the Bible: Studying it with your mind made up or studying it to let it make up your mind."*
~ Author Unknown

Delighting in God's Word

"But his delight is in the law of the LORD, and on his law he meditates day and night" (Psalm 1:2 NIV).

Here the psalmist is referring to godly people whose hearts and minds are focused on the things of God. What in your life brings you the most joy—the most delight? We live in a world focused on material things and satisfying our physical appetites as the means to bring us complete happiness. As believers, we can easily be drawn into seeking fulfillment and joy somewhere other than in our relationship with our Lord.

In our passage, we see that the source of delight to the godly is in the Word of the Lord. How can this be? Isn't it strange that, in our selfish world, a simple book of paper and ink could be the source of such pleasure and fulfillment? The more we delight in studying and obeying God's Word, the more fruitful we will become.

On the other hand, the more we allow the values of a world that ridicules God to affect our thoughts and attitudes, the more we separate ourselves from our source of spiritual nourishment and inexplicable peace and joy.

We experience delightful lives when we become so closely related to God that we find pleasure in the habitual, daily study of God's revelation of Himself—the Word. Back to my question: "What in your life brings you the most joy?" If God's Word is not a joy to you, perhaps you are a tourist rather than an explorer.

"There is a basic difference between an explorer and a tourist.

The tourist travels quickly, stopping only to observe the highly noticeable or publicized points of interest. The explorer, on the other hand, takes his time to search out all that he can find. Too many of us read the Bible like a tourist and then complain that our devotional times are fruitless. It is necessary that we take time to explore the Bible. Then notable nooks and crannies will appear as we get beneath the surface." ~ Unknown Author

We can literally hear the awesome voice of God in His Word through which He reveals truths about Himself, including His character, love, and will to those who delight in Him. Remember, *"All Scripture is God-breathed and is useful to teach us what is true and to make us realize what is wrong in our lives"* (2 Timothy 3:16 NIV).

Jul 16

Chuckle: *"If you saw a lawyer and an IRS agent drowning and you could only save one of them, would you go to lunch or read the newspaper?"*

Quote: *"The circumstances of a saint's life are ordained by God. All our circumstances are in the hand of God, therefore never think it strange concerning the circumstances you are in."*
~ Oswald Chambers

Disappointment with God

"And we know that God causes everything to work together for the good of those who love God and are called according to his purpose for them" (Romans 8:29 NLT).

Let's face it, life is full of disappointments. Sometimes we are even disappointed with God because He doesn't do as we expect Him to do, want Him to do, or think He should do. When it comes to disappointment with God, please remember that God does not conduct Himself by our standards, but rather by what is best for us as He carries out His plan for our lives. God says, *"For my thoughts are not your thoughts, neither are your ways my ways"* (Isaiah 55:8 NIV).

We should, however, bring our disappointments to God in prayer and be honest with Him. After all, He knows our thoughts anyway, so there's no point in trying to hide them.

You may not always understand why God allows pain to come into your life, but consider that God may be trying to teach you and work His power through you in those circumstances. When you are disappointed with God, it's a good idea to ask God: "Lord, what are you trying to teach me through this experience?"

In our disappointments, it's important that we move toward God, not away from Him. Getting angry with God and running from the very one who can help you through your pain is not the way of the spiritually wise. *"O God, you are my God; I earnestly search for you.*

My soul thirsts for you" (Psalm 63:1 NLT). Listen to and trust God, even when it seems to make no sense.

You can reduce, or eliminate, disappointment with God by putting Him first in your life. When we make self all-important, we are setting ourselves up for God to disappoint us. But when He is first, our goal is to please Him, not ourselves. Then it becomes much easier for us to understand God's ways and His intentions. *"As the Scriptures express it, 'I am placing a stone in Jerusalem, a chosen cornerstone, and anyone who believes in him will never be disappointed'"* (1 Peter 2:6 NLT).

To believe in Christ means to have faith in Him, to trust Him, and commit our lives to Him. As we place our complete trust in the Lord, our expectations of Him will change. As our creator, He knows what is best for us, and we can learn from Him as He reveals to us His master-plans for our lives. *"Give your burdens to the Lord, and he will take care of you"* (Psalm 55:22 NLT).

Jul 17

Chuckle: Church Bulletin blooper: *"Barbara remains in the hospital. She is having trouble sleeping and requests CD's of Pastor Jack's sermons."*

Quote: *"The Lord disciplines those he loves." How petty our complaining is! Our Lord begins to bring us into the place where we can have communion with Him, and we groan and say, "O Lord, let me be like other people!"* ~ Oswald Chambers

God's Loving Discipline

"My child, don't ignore it when the Lord disciplines you, and don't be discouraged when he corrects you. For the Lord disciplines those he loves, and he punishes those he accepts as children" (Hebrews 12:5b-6 NLT).

When we find ourselves in troublesome situations, it's popular to blame Satan. We may think Satan is waging spiritual warfare against us when we experience unpleasant circumstances and hardships. It's so much easier to blame our troubles on Satan than to admit we may be reaping what we have sown (see Galatians 6:7), and are being chastised and disciplined by our loving Heavenly Father.

We all know there have been times when we were guilty of not listening to God—not paying attention to what His Word was saying. For some of us, God may have used severe discipline to get our attention so that we would restore our fellowship with Him and once again listen for and obey His voice.

Who do you think loves his child the most—the parent who allows his child to make his own bad choices and make mistakes that will ultimately harm him, or the parent who shows love by disciplining his child with correction, training, and even appropriate punishment? I think the answer is obvious.

We can mistake our difficulties for the work of Satan, when in fact they are the result of a loving God warning us of looming dangers because of sin in our lives. No doubt God disciplines us to get us back on the right path. How sad it is when a child of God never makes the connection between life's problems and God's loving discipline.

"No discipline is enjoyable while it is happening—it is painful! But afterward there will be a quiet harvest of right living for those who are trained in this way" (Hebrews 12:11 NLT).

God's discipline is never pleasant, but it is an unmistakable sign of God's perfect love and concern for us. One thing is certain, because of God's love for you, His discipline will be for your ultimate good.

Our most important question should be: What is God trying to teach me through His disciplining?

Jul 18

Chuckle: *I ate one time at a Pizzeria. That's a weird name. Sounds more like something you would get from eating bad pizza!"*

Quote: *"Revenge, at first though sweet, Bitter ere long back on itself recoils."* ~ John Milton

An Eye for An Eye

"You have heard that the law of Moses says, 'If an eye is injured, injure the eye of the person who did it. If a tooth gets knocked out, knock out the tooth of the person who did it. But I say, don't resist an evil person! If you are slapped on the right cheek, turn the other too" (Matthew 5:38-39 NLT).

For as long as I can remember, I have heard the phrase: "An eye for an eye and a tooth for a tooth." The phrase has its origin in the law that was given by God to the judges of the Old Testament. In effect, the law said: "Make the punishment fit the crime." Although it was not intended to approve the exacting of revenge on someone, some were using it to justify vendettas against other people. To this day, people try to justify their acts of reprisal and revenge with words like, "I was just treating him the way he treated me."

It's a human tendency to want to "get even" when we are wronged. Jesus understood how dangerous such attitudes could be to the harmony among His people. It's no different today.

Jesus says we are to do good to those who do us wrong. He even tells us we are to love our enemies. We are not to keep score but to love and forgive. I don't need to tell you that this is an unnatural reaction—it is a supernatural reaction. As Christians, we must recognize that only God can provide us the strength and will to love and forgive as He does. When someone does an evil thing to you, Jesus would have us pray for the perpetrator, rather than planning vengeance.

Jesus continues: *"If you are ordered to court and your shirt is taken from you, give your coat, too. If a soldier demands that you carry his gear for a mile, carry it two miles. Give to those who ask, and don't turn away from those who want to borrow"* (Matthew 5:40-42 NLT).

The Jews of Jesus' day were no different than people today—they found these statements offensive and unacceptable. Any Messiah who would turn the other cheek was not the military leader they wanted to lead a revolt against Rome. They hated their Roman oppressors and wanted retaliation against them. And wouldn't you know it, along came Jesus with this radical and senseless response to injustice.

Instead of demanding our rights, He wants us to give them up freely without rancor or bitterness. The message from our Lord is that it is much more important to give justice and mercy than it is to receive justice ourselves. Wow! What a concept!

By displaying Christ-like love and kindness to those who offend us, we can overcome evil with good. Forgiveness and kindness are much more powerful weapons than revenge and anger.

The next time someone treats you wrongly, stop and think about this teaching—count to ten or 100, whatever it takes—then return love and kindness. You may be surprised at the reaction of the one who receives undeserved love and forgiveness. After all, isn't that what Jesus did for us?

Jul 19

Chuckle: *"Children are like mosquitos: the minute they stop making a noise, you know they're getting into something."*
Quote: *"Faith fills a man with love for the beauty of its truth, with faith in the truth of its beauty."* ~ St Francis de Sales.

Faith of a Child

Then Jesus prayed this prayer, *"O Father, Lord of heaven and earth, thank you for hiding the truth from those who think themselves so wise and clever, and for revealing it to the childlike. Yes, Father, it pleased you to do it this way!"* (Matthew 11:25 NLT).

Words spoken by Jesus Himself penetrate our hearts and minds in extraordinary ways. His words in our passage are no different. Here Jesus mentions two kinds of people in His prayer:

First, those who see themselves as learned, wise, and clever—arrogant in their own knowledge and wisdom, and second, those who approach God with a humble faith like that of a little child—open to receive the truth of God's Word.

To hear our Lord praying these words to His Father should cause each of us to examine our motives, priorities, and where we are placing our trust. How do you see yourself—as wise and self-sufficient? Or as one who seeks God's truth with humble, childlike faith, realizing that only God holds all the answers to our questions about life and eternity?

In His teachings, Jesus often contrasted the believing wise and the foolish unbelievers and emphasized a need to become wise through a simple faith like that of a little child. Here are additional words from Jesus. *". . . I assure you, unless you turn from your sins and become as little children, you will never get into the Kingdom of Heaven. Therefore, anyone who becomes humble as this little child is the greatest in the Kingdom of Heaven"* (Matthew 18:3-4 NLT).

These words should cause each of us to fall on our knees and ask forgiveness for our arrogance, self-centeredness, and self-serving attitudes. Children are, by nature, innocent and trusting, and Jesus used a child to help His self-centered disciples understand His teaching point. We are to be humble with sincere hearts—not childish in our actions but with childlike faith.

"When a father picks up his little daughter and tosses her into the air, she laughs and enjoys it, for she trusts—has faith in—her father. Even though she finds herself in unusual situations, like being upside down four feet above the floor with nothing supporting her, normally a most uncomfortable circumstance, she does not fear, for she trusts her father. That is the sort of faith we should have toward our heavenly Father, too." ~ Illustrations for Biblical Preaching; Edited by Michael P. Green

Jul 20

Chuckle: *A reporter asked a 103-year-old woman, "And what is the best thing about being 103?"*

She simply replied, "No peer pressure."

Quote: *"Physical strength can never permanently withstand the impact of spiritual force." ~ Franklin D. Roosevelt.*

Fighting Against God

"So my advice is, leave these men alone. If they are teaching and doing things merely on their own, it will soon be overthrown. But if it is of God, you will not be able to stop them. You may even find yourselves fighting against God" (Acts 5:38-39 NLT).

I read somewhere that more people have been killed for their Christian faith in the last century than in all previous history. Living here in the relative safety of our beloved USA, this may sound preposterous.

However, millions of Christians around the world practice their faith in the face of grave dangers, including imprisonment, torture, or even death. The threat is real and the persecution is real in this modern day. You may have, as I have, participated in offerings for the persecuted church to buy Bibles and other Christian materials for struggling Christians around the world.

It's interesting to study how the early church flourished in the face of severe persecution, while today many of our churches are floundering in decline with little or no threat of persecution. But God continues to open people's hearts to the gospel in places where new Christians know that suffering awaits them.

In our passage, members of the powerful Jewish Sanhedrin were persecuting Peter and the apostles for preaching the gospel message. One wise Sanhedrin member, Gamaliel, told his companions that if the gospel message of Peter and the apostles was of God, no amount of persecution would be able to stop the movement, and they might even find themselves fighting against

God.

    As I read this passage, and thought about the persecution of early Christians, the question came to my mind: How faithful would I be to Christ and His church if I faced a threat of arrest when I stepped outside my place of worship? In many places around the world our fellow believers face such threats every day, but yet they remain faithful.

    "There is no place for fear among men and women who serve the Almighty, who do not hesitate to humble themselves in seeking divine guidance through prayer. Though persecutions arise, though reverses come, in prayer we can find reassurance, for God will speak peace to the soul. That peace, that spirit of serenity, is life's greatest blessing. ~ Ezra Taft Benson

    Those who persecute Christians are fighting against God and will never be successful in quenching the fires of faith in Jesus Christ and in His church. However, we must remain faithful so there will be no doubt that what we preach, teach, and live are consistent with God's Word and His will.

    Let's fight against evil, and be sure not to fight against God.

Jul 21

Chuckle: *"When an egotist gets up in the morning and puts his pants on, he thinks the whole world is dressed!"*

Quote: *"If we open a quarrel between the past and the present, we shall find that we have lost the future."* ~ Winston Churchill

Confidence in the Future

"And I am sure that God, who began the good work within you, will continue his work until it is finally finished on that day when Christ Jesus comes back again" (Philippians 1:6 NLT).

Here Paul expresses his confidence about the future. He drew the conclusion that God was at work in the Philippian Christians and that He would complete His work. God's faithfulness made him certain. Paul's love for them made him confident. And the Philippian Christian's faithfulness made it sure. This passage does not mean their salvation was incomplete, but that God would continue to work in their lives to make them the kind of Christians He wanted them to be—to make them more like Jesus.

We are God's work in progress. Paul knew that God loves finished works, and that God's plans do not fail. The Greek word translated *"being confident/sure"* denotes personal certainty. The "good work" refers to the "partnership in the gospel" mentioned in verse 5. God's work in them was not yet complete. He would continue it until it was fulfilled according to His eternal plan and will. God's faithfulness guarantees the completion of what He begins. The same is true as God works in your life and mine.

The day when Christ comes back suggests a day of victory and of trial when every Christian's work/deeds will be tested. It will be a time of victory, celebration, and reward for the faithful Christian, and a time of disappointment and shame for the Christian who has not been faithful to his/her Lord in this life. Also, the completion of His good work of grace, which will consummate our eternal salvation, will occur in the day Jesus returns in victory. After that, every Christian will stand before the judgment seat of Christ, where his works will be judged (see 2 Corinthians 5:10).

Paul expresses a personal confidence in the faithfulness in his Lord this way: "... *I know whom I have believed, and am convinced that he is able to guard what I have entrusted to him for that day*" (2 Timothy 1:12 NIV). The present evil age will come to an end with the second coming of Christ, the Day of the Lord.

"In the choir of life, it's easy to fake the words—but someday each of us will have to sing solo before God." ~ Unknown Author

Jul 22

Chuckle: A child's prayer: *"Dear God, I like the story about Noah the best of all of them. You really made up some good ones. I like walking on water, too."* ~ Glenn

Quote: *"We live by encouragement and die without it—slowly, sadly, angrily."* ~ Celeste Holm

Encourage Someone Today

"And let us consider how we may spur (stimulate) one another on toward love and good deeds. Let us not give up meeting together, as some are in the habit of doing, but let us encourage one another...." (Hebrews 10:24-25 NIV).

There may be issues in your life that cause you to need a pat on the back, an understanding hug, a knowing look, or a word of encouragement. You may feel as if the good things you do for others go unnoticed and unappreciated. We all experience these kinds of feelings and needs from time to time. And when we do, isn't it wonderful to have a sensitive person respond to our need with the right gesture at just the right time?

How would you define the word "encouragement?" It seems to me that it is something we do that inspires others to have renewed courage, spirit, or hope. By encouraging someone, we stimulate and affirm him/her as a person of value. It's important to note the distinction between appreciation and affirmation. Appreciation is expressed as a result of something accomplished. However, affirmation encourages by addressing the value of the person. Most of us need both affirmation and appreciation.

If I were to ask you why Christians assemble for a worship service, how would you answer? You might say: "to participate in life-changing worship through the singing of hymns, praying, giving tithes and offerings, hearing inspirational music, and finally, listening to a helpful sermon." Although these answers are accurate, there is another important reason which should be included. Our Scripture passage will help us to discover that reason—to encourage one another.

In the early church, persecution was prevalent and martyrdom was commonplace. As a result, fear gripped the hearts of individual believers and whole congregations. Some defected, others drifted away to safety.

A letter began to circulate among the Christian Jews addressing those who persevered and endured the persecution. Today we know that letter as Hebrews. The writer understood the value of people coming together for worship and fellowship. He warned them not to compromise their beliefs and then informed them of the importance of those times they spent together, as follows:

- Let us seriously consider how to stimulate one another   (vs. 24)
- Let us faithfully assemble ourselves together (vs. 25)
- Let us <u>encourage one another</u> (vs. 25)—the major point of   this passage.

I read somewhere that "encouragement is like a peanut butter sandwich—the more you spread it around, the better things stick together." Encouraging one another is a major responsibility of each Christian. Let's encourage someone today.

Jul 23

Chuckle: *Parachute recall notice: On page 7 of the instruction manual, please change the words 'state zip code" to "Pull rip cord*

Quote: *"There is nothing better than the encouragement of a good friend."* ~ Katherine Butler Hathaway

Worship and Encouragement

"Let us not give up meeting together, as some are in the habit of doing, but let us encourage one another—and all the more as you see the Day approaching" (Hebrews 10:25 NIV).

We may attend church services out of devotion to our Lord, to participate in worship, to pray, to enjoy the beautiful music, and to hear a relevant sermon. These are all appropriate reasons for faithful attendance which benefit us greatly. But have you thought about how your presence encourages others?

Notice what God's Word says:

~ *"Not forsaking"* is the more clear KJV rendering. The call of these words is for faithfulness in common worship and fellowship. Here God issues a solemn warning against setting a bad example by abandoning public worship. The active Christian life, inspired by love, is kept alive and growing by people who care enough for their Lord and one another to assemble together.

~ *"Encouraging one another"* reminds each of us to consider the discouragement we bring to the Christian church when we deliberately remove ourselves from its services. We see there is much more to worship than listening to a sermon and saying a prayer, as important as these things are.

In this passage is more evidence that God is interested in having our relationship with Him borne out by the way we relate to other people. Encouraging one another should be a major objective every time we come together, as well as other times when we make contact.

I have heard people say, "I'm a Christian and have a close

relationship with the Lord, but I can maintain that relationship without attending church." Or "I can worship the Lord without attending church." Of course we can worship God other than in a corporate worship service, but it is God's plan and instruction that we should not neglect coming together.

In addition to worshiping God, the interpersonal relationships which are developed provide a source of encouragement, even in the worst of times. Relationships are strengthened, fellowship becomes warmer, and mutual encouragement becomes a powerful force in the lives of worshipers.

I've heard people say "it doesn't matter which church I go to," when they really meant, "it doesn't really matter which church I stay home from!"

How about you? If you are already a faithful church attendee, then consider this an affirmation of your faithfulness. If not, perhaps it has given you another reason to be faithful—to be an encourager. Your faithful participation in worship services serves as a witness to your devotion to our Lord.

Chuckle: Child's prayer: *"God, did you really mean for a giraffe to look like that or was it an accident?"* Norma

Quote: *"Everyone who has ever done a kind deed for us, or spoken a word of encouragement to us, has entered into the make-up of our character and our thoughts, as well as our success."* ~ George Matthew Adams

Becoming an Encourager

"Therefore encourage one another and build each other up, just as in fact you are doing" (1 Thessalonians 5:11).

The art of being an encourager is not an innate ability—it must be developed. The virtue is first developed and cultivated in the home. Children learn it up from their parents as they hear words of love, affirmation, praise, and approval.

Sadly, all homes are not like that. Evangelist Bill Glass once asked a group of prison inmates, "How many of you had parents who told you you would end up in prison?" Almost every one of the inmates raised his hand. No encouragement there. . . .!

Now back to Hebrews 10:24: *"we are to consider how to stimulate one another to love and good deeds."* We are to give thought to specific ways we can lift up, affirm, and help others. God's commands are not theoretical—they are for specific, practical application, especially those that relate to people in need.

Here are some examples:

- Tell someone how much they mean to you—how he or she blesses your life
- Observe and mention admirable character qualities you see in others
- Correspond with others through calls, thank you notes, etc.
- Notice and comment on something done well by

others
- Cultivate a positive and reassuring attitude—be a source of optimism and cheer
- Be supportive of someone who is hurting—a hug, a kind word, a note, etc.
- Help someone strengthen his or her faith

"And we urge you, brothers (sisters), warn those who are idle, encourage the timid, help the weak, be patient with everyone" (1 Thessalonians 5:14 NIV). We must be careful to be encouragers with no thought of getting anything in return. If we selfishly expect something in return, our attempts at being an encourager will result in giving guilt-trips rather than encouragement.

Here is a summary of Hebrews 10:25 from the Life Application Study Bible: *"To neglect Christian meetings is to give up the encouragement and help of other Christians. We gather together to share our faith and to strengthen (encourage) one another in the Lord. As we get closer to the day when Christ will return, we will face many spiritual struggles, and even times of persecution. Anti-Christian forces will grow in strength. Difficulties should never be excuses for missing church services. Rather, as difficulties arise, we should make an even greater effort to be faithful in attendance."* By our faithfulness, we will be encouraged and also encourage others.

You may not be physically able to attend worship services. If so, you can still be an encourager by maintaining contact with other Christians who need encouragement.

Jul 25

Chuckle: *A young couple invited their elderly pastor for Sunday dinner. While they were in the kitchen preparing the meal, the minister asked their son what they were having. "Goat," the little boy replied.*

"Goat?" replied the startled man of the cloth, "Are you sure about that?"

"Yep," said the youngster. "I heard Dad say to Mom, 'Today is just as good as any to have the old goat for dinner.'"

Quote: *"There are high spots in all of our lives and most of them have come about through encouragement from someone else."* ~ Unknown Source

Encouragement and the Holy Spirit

"But the Counselor, the Holy Spirit, whom the Father will send in my name, will teach you all things and will remind you of everything I have said to you" (John 14:26 NIV).

The word for "encourage" in Hebrews 10:25 (NIV translation) is from the same Greek word used for the "Holy Spirit" in John 14:26. In each case it means "helper." The word literally means "one called alongside to be our companion and to help us."

Being an encourager is as close as we can come to doing the work of the Holy Spirit. What a thrilling blessing it is to know we have been called alongside someone to help them. If all of us could grasp the significance of being an encourager, there's no limit to what God could do through us to stimulate one another as Christians—what we could accomplish for our Lord.

Being an encourager to others is among the highest and most important privileges any of us can have. It is easy to pour cold water on someone's enthusiasm, excitement, and optimism. It is easy to discourage others, and the world is full of discouragers. But we have a Christian responsibility to encourage one another. Many a time a word of praise or thanks or appreciation or cheer has kept a person on his or her feet.

Any of us can be an encourager if we have allowed God to put in our hearts just an extra measure of love, concern, and understanding. God will give you the skills you need. However, it does take a large measure of compassion and commitment to be an encourager. A brother or sister may be withering on the vine spiritually and emotionally for lack of affirmation and encouragement. They may be suffering from feelings of loneliness, inadequacy, and worthlessness. Feelings of worth are fostered by encouragement.

Some need encouragement to attend church with us. After all, God instructs us as to its value. *"Let us not give up meeting . . . but let us encourage one another. . . ."* (Hebrews 10:25 NIV). Those who have fallen out of the fellowship need someone to show them the way back—to encourage them. You can be the Holy Spirit's mouthpiece to lift the spirits of those who need someone to care.

Please join me in praying that God will direct our paths to someone who needs encouragement, and that He will give us the courage and concern to meet that need.

Chuckle: *A man writing to the meteorologist: "I thought you may be interested in knowing that I shoveled eighteen inches of 'partly cloudy' from my sidewalk this morning."*

Quote: *"Blessed is he who does good to others and desires not that others should do him good."* ~ Br Giles *Little Flowers of St Francis*

Spirit of the Golden Rule

"In everything, do to others what you would have them do to you, for this sums up the law and the prophets" (Matthew 7:12 NIV).

Near the end of His Sermon on the Mount, Jesus introduced His famous Golden Rule. Unlike similar sayings by other Jewish teachers, Jesus stated the rule in a positive way—by telling us what to do rather than what not to do. This rule represents the very essence of Jesus' teaching concerning human relationships. He wants us to apply the principles of this rule by positive actions toward others in the same way we want others to treat us. However, our desire to have others do good to us should not be our motivation for doing good. Our motivation should be our obedience to our Lord along with genuine love and concern for others. Our quote for today says it quite well.

The Golden Rule provides the basis for how we should relate to other people—that is, unless we distort its meaning to fit our selfish and self-centered attitude. Sometimes, mainly in jest, I've heard it stated like this: "Do unto others before they do it unto you." Or "do unto others as they do unto you." These tongue-in-cheek distortions of the Golden Rule seem to describe the attitudes of some in our selfish, greedy, and materialistic society. If we care only for ourselves, we violate the spirit of the Golden Rule by our unconcern for others.

It is relatively easy to refrain from harming others, but much more difficult to take the initiative and do something good and uplifting for them. Remember, these are the words of Jesus—His

Golden Rule. As He formulated it, He described the very foundation of genuine goodness and mercy. It's not possible to live by the Rule unless we love others with the kind of love God shows to us every day. As we study the Golden Rule together, I'm sure God would have each of us to think of someone whom we can bless today by good, kind, and merciful actions that demonstrate our love.

No doubt the way we relate to others will determine how we are treated. God is pleased when we treat our brothers and sisters with love and compassion, regardless of how they treat us in return.

"It takes a long time to fill a glass with drops of water. Even when the glass seems full, it can still take one, two, three, four, or five or more additional drops. But if you will keep at it, there is at last that one drop that makes the glass overflow. The same applies to deeds of kindness. In a series of kindnesses there is at last one that makes the heart run over." ~ Illustrations for Biblical Preaching; Edited by Michael P. Green

Jul 27

Chuckle: *Hearing her young son open the front door, a mother shouted, "Be careful on that floor, Jimmy; it's just been waxed."*

Walking right in, Jimmy replied, "Don't worry, Mom, I'm wearing my cleats."

Quote: *"It is good for us to think that no grace or blessing is truly ours till we are aware that God has blessed someone else with it through us."* ~ Phillips Brooks

Abounding Grace

"And God is able to make all grace abound to you, so that in all things at all times, having all that you need, you will abound in every good work" (2 Corinthians 9:8 NIV).

A few years back, I received an e-mail from Dayspring Devotions in which they emphasized the wonderful acts of God's grace toward each of us every day we live as Christians. I will quote them before providing some commentary of my own.

"Grace. What a wonderful word! The very sound of it brings health and healing, comfort and reassurance, encouragement and hope. What does this wonderful word mean to us who have trusted in Christ? What is Grace? Here are some helpful and wonderful definitions that have been written and spoken through the years:

*Grace is **G**od's **R**iches **A**t **C**hrist's **E**xpense.*

Grace is God's unmerited favor.

Grace is God working in us the will and desire to do the things that please him. Grace is receiving from God what we do not deserve, freely, without money or price. Grace is God's influence upon us resulting in happiness and thankfulness."

Any strength we may possess that lets us pattern our lives after Jesus, by showing unearned and undeserved love, is given to us by God Himself. There is nothing we can do to make ourselves worthy of receiving God's grace because if we earned it, we would deserve it, and grace, by its very nature, is that which we do not deserve.

"For it is by grace you have been saved through faith . . ." (Ephesians 2:8 NIV). Our very salvation and eternal life are gifts from God—by His grace. *"Amazing Grace, how sweet the sound, that saved a wretch like me . . ."* This undeserved grace is a function of God's love and mercy. We just need to accept God's free grace gift, then allow His grace to work through us. It is this work of God that motivates us to work for Him for His glory and the good of others.

During the Spanish-American War, Theodore Roosevelt came to Clara Barton of the Red Cross to buy some supplies for his sick and wounded men. His request was refused. Roosevelt was troubled and asked, "How can I get these things? I must have proper food for my sick men." "Just ask for them, Colonel," said Barton. "Oh," said Roosevelt, "then I do ask for them." He got them at once through grace, not through purchase. ~ Illustrations for Biblical Preaching; Edited by Michael P. Green

Jul 28

Chuckle: *A kind woman watched a small boy as he tried to reach the doorbell of a house. Thinking she should help, she walked up and rang it for him. "Okay, what now?" the woman asked the boy.*
"Run like crazy," he answered. "That's what I'm gonna do!"

Quote: *"Costly grace is the treasure hidden in the field; for the sake of it a man will gladly go and sell all that he has. It is costly because it costs a man his life, and it is grace because it gives a man the only true life."* ~ Dietrich Bonhoeffer

God's Never Ending Grace

"The Word (Jesus) became flesh and made his dwelling among us. We have seen his glory, the glory of the One and Only, who came from the Father, full of grace and truth ... From the fullness of his grace we have all received (one) blessing (grace) after another" (John 1:14, 16 NIV).

God's grace is an amazing attribute of His character. Literally, "grace" is getting what we do not deserve—or more than we deserve. Grace should not be confused with "mercy," which is not getting what we deserve, or "justice," which is getting what we deserve. Initially, it is God's grace whereby we are saved: *"For it is by grace you have been saved, through faith— and this not from yourselves, it is the gift of God—not by works, so that no one can boast"* (Ephesians 2:8-9 NIV).

As important as God's grace is for our salvation, there is much more of His grace available to us every single day. Remember, God wants each of us to experience a life full of joy and peace. He wants us to have the absolute best and fullest life that only He can give us (see John 10:10).

In our basic passage, we are told that Jesus came full of grace and truth. God's "grace" springs from His never-ending, boundless love and generosity. "Truth," on the other hand, stresses God's determination to be consistent, reliable, predictable, and trustworthy in His dealings with us. You can trust all the promises of God recorded in His Word. You can take them to the bank, so to speak. Grace without truth would make it meaningless. In declaring the character of God, Jesus combined an infinite tenderness toward us, as sinful people, with an unswerving fidelity and faithfulness.

Notice that God gives us His grace followed by even more grace one portion of grace after another. The flow of God's grace is like the waves of the ocean. One wave of grace is followed by another wave of grace over and over again. God's grace is never ending. Once the gift of God's grace is received, it never stops flowing and growing.

God wants us to be conscious of His grace and draw upon it daily for strength, peace, and comfort. And, as the God of truth, He wants us to trust Him implicitly and rely upon His promises. Promises like: *"Never will I leave you; never will I forsake you"* (Hebrews 13:5b NIV), or *"I am with you always, to the very end of the age"* (Matthew 28:20b NIV).

Jul 29

Chuckle: *When I was little, I often wondered who Richard Stands was. You know: "I pledge allegiance to the flag . . . And to the republic for Richard Stands."*

Quote: *"If it were our lot to suffer deprivation, as it is the lot of many in the world, then gratitude for the little things of life and the big things of God would come more readily to our lips."*
~ Cardinal Basil Hume

Gracious Gratitude

"One of them (the healed lepers), when he saw that he was healed, came back to Jesus, shouting, 'Praise God, I'm healed!' He fell face down on the ground at Jesus' feet, thanking him for what he had done. The man was a Samaritan" (Luke 17:16 NLT).

I think there are basically three ways we can react when being offered a free gift from God or another person: We can refuse the gift for fear of obligating ourselves to the giver. We can accept the gift while we see ourselves as worthy, entitled, and deserving because of our circumstances or who we are. Or we can accept the gift while seeing ourselves as unworthy and undeserving as our hearts are filled with humility, praise, and gratitude.

I'm sure you are familiar with the story leading up to our passage where Jesus healed ten lepers, but only one, a Samaritan, showed gratitude to Jesus for what had been done for him. This account reminds us that it is very possible to receive God's wondrous gifts while harboring an ungrateful attitude in our hearts. Nine of the ten lepers never received the blessing of hearing Jesus say, *"Stand up and go. Your faith has made you well"* (vs. 19).

When we are grateful for what God does for us, we grow spiritually and become more like Jesus, our ultimate role model for Christian living. We grow in our understanding of God's wonderful grace and mercy as we express our gratitude. God uses our response as an opportunity to teach us more about Himself.

Lastly, this passage teaches us that God's love, grace, and mercy are for everyone, regardless of race or social status. The Samaritans were despised by the Jews, who saw themselves as the only pure descendants of Abraham. The hated Samaritans were a mixed race from the intermarriage between Jews and other people after Israel's exile.

The Jews looked down their noses at the Samaritans and would not associate with them in any way. It must have been most difficult for the Jews to accept, but the Samaritan's gratitude for Jesus healing him taught them and us a valuable lesson—that God does not discriminate when bestowing His love, grace, and mercy. He loves every human being equally.

Christ died for the sins of all and He is deserving of our deepest gratitude.

Jul 30

Chuckle: *Q: What was one of the first things Adam and Eve did after they were kicked out of the of the Garden? A: They really raised Cain.*

Quote: *"The 'heart' in the biblical sense is not inward life, but the whole man in relation to God."* ~ Dietrich Bonhoeffer

A Heart Condition

"Create in me a clean heart, O God. Renew a right spirit within me" (Psalm 51:10 NLT). *"May the words of my mouth and the thoughts of my heart be pleasing to you, O Lord, my rock and my redeemer"* (Psalm 19:14 NLT).

When a reader shared with me that these two verses of Scripture are her prayers, I began to reflect anew on God's desires concerning our hearts. I was reminded that the word "heart" in Scripture warrants our study to understand its exact meaning. We know that *"Man looks at the outward appearance, but the Lord looks at the heart"* (1 Samuel 16:7 NIV).

The word "heart" does not refer to the vital organ in our chests that pumps blood to keep us alive. It means much more than that. The word refers to the very core, or center, of our lives. As your physical heart is the center of your physical body, your spiritual heart is the center of your spiritual life. The heart includes our intellect, will, emotions, passions, appetites, morals, thoughts, spirit— the totality of our being.

If we see the heart in this light, this Great Commandment from the lips of Jesus becomes more meaningful: *"Love the Lord your God with all your heart and with all your soul and with all your mind and with all your strength"* (Mark 12:30 NIV).

C. Ryder Smith says this commandment could better be rendered, *"Love the Lord your God with all your heart—that is all your soul, mind, and strength."* When stated like this, we see that the heart includes all these other dimensions of our being.

When we allow God to give us a clean heart, everything about us becomes clean—our words, our actions, our thoughts. We give everything we are, have, think, and do over to Him. When our hearts are cleansed, our spirit becomes right with God and even our thoughts (meditations) become acceptable to God. When God truly gives us a new heart, our lives are transformed into the image of Christ. For this to happen, we can't hold anything back from God's cleansing power.

"If we confess our sins, he is faithful and just and will forgive our sins and purify (cleanse) us from all unrighteousness" (1 John 1:9 NIV). When we allow God to cleanse us from all unrighteousness, everything about us is washed clean. When our hearts are clean, our worship will be acceptable and pleasing to God.

Chuckle: *"It's a good thing I found you, Gideon. It seems someone has been hiding all your Bibles in motel rooms."*

Quote: *"The human soul is like a bird that is born in a cage. Nothing can deprive it of its natural longings, or obliterate the mysterious remembrance of its heritage."* ~ Epes Sargent

Our Christian Heritage

"Listen to me, all who hope for deliverance—all who seek the Lord! Consider the quarry from which you were mined, the rock from which you were cut" (Isaiah 51:1 NLT).

It seems the older I get the more interested I become in my family history. I'm thankful for Christian family members who have gone on to be with the Lord, and my living elderly relatives have become even more precious to me. I often think about the Christian heritage they have given me, and I reflect on their faithfulness in years past.

Living in the past can be dangerous to your emotional health if overdone. However, a healthy respect for those who made your life possible and more meaningful is good and proper. As believers, we do well to stop and think of all the faithful Christians who have gone before us and the great heritage they have left us. We should never overlook our history because it helps us to understand who we are and gives us a sense of purpose—where God is leading us.

At the time of Isaiah's writings, God's people had forgotten what God had done for them. They had also forgotten about their faithful, spiritual ancestors such as Abraham, Moses, Isaac, and Jacob. They were living as spiritual paupers rather than heirs to a wonderful heritage as members of God's royal priesthood—as God's people. The call in our passage suggests the vital need for all Christians to focus their hearts and minds on the underlying principles which characterize our faith.

Today, as a Christian, you enjoy an even richer heritage than did the people in Isaiah's day. We have the broad shoulders of great New Testament Christians—like Peter, John, and Paul—to stand on and to draw strength from. You may also have come from a Christian family whose faithfulness to Christ goes back many generations. If so, you are most fortunate. We should view our heritage as a special gift of God and be forever thankful.

The key questions for you and me are: What kind of heritage am I leaving for my children and generations to come? Will they look back with thanksgiving for the life I lived and the Christian instruction I provided them? These are sobering questions that we would be wise to deal with right now.

Now is a great time for life assessment by each of us as a parent or grandparent. If we Christians—even a faithful few—remain steadfast, just think what God can do through us to inspire and influence current and future generations.

Aug 01

Chuckle: *"In an interview, Donald Trump says he uses Head & Shoulders on his hair. As a result, Head & Shoulders is suing Trump for slander."* ~ Conan O'Brien

Quote: *"Jesus Christ is the key which unlocks the door of the prison cell of our own making and sets us free to live in the wide world of God's love and purpose."* ~ Kenneth Pillar

Hold Your Head High

"I have set you free; now walk with your heads held high" (Leviticus 26:13 NIV). *"So if the Son sets you free, you will be free indeed"* (John 8:36 NIV).

Have you taken a moment recently to reflect anew on the glorious truth that, as a born again child of God, you have been set free from the bondage of sin, anxiety, fear, and guilt? You are no longer a captive of the things of this world, and you can rejoice because of what God has done for you through Christ.

In our passage, God wants all His people to live like we have been set free and to hold our heads up high, not in arrogance or smugness, but with confidence and rejoicing. He wants us to be filled with joy and thanksgiving, and never allow anything to diminish this joy.

Just think what it must be like for a slave laborer to be set free. Our passage reminds us that God brought the children of Israel out of centuries of slavery and gave them freedom and dignity. We too are set free when we accept, through faith, Christ's ultimate sacrificial gift that redeems us from the slavery of sin.

We can now walk with confidence and dignity because, not only has God forgiven us of our sins, but has completely forgotten that we were ever in the bondage of sin. *"I, even I, am he who blots out your transgressions, for my own sake, and remembers your sins no more"* (Isaiah 23:25 NIV).

Yes, God sets us free because He loves us, but He has another purpose too. He wants us to use this freedom for His glory and to inspire the highest level of righteousness within us. He wants us to grow more like Jesus each day as His Word teaches us and His Holy Spirit guides us, convicts us, and strengthens us.

God knows that the greatest security and happiness His people can enjoy comes from our living in close fellowship with Him. With an omnipotent God who has our best interests at heart, we can face even the most discouraging situations with confidence, joy, and hope. We can walk with our heads held high. PRAISE!

Aug 02

Chuckle: *A pastor asked some young children where they wanted to go when they die. "To heaven," they all piped up.*
"And what do you have to do to get there," asked the pastor.
"Be dead!" shouted one little boy.
Quote: *"Christ can give us the courage to pick up the broken pieces of life, to put them back together, and start over again."*
~ William Ward

A Pure Heart

"Create in me a clean, pure, heart, O God. Renew a right spirit within me" (Psalm 51:10 NLT).

Psalm 51 was written by King David to express his great remorse and repentance for the terrible sins he had committed. He knew his actions had brought great pain to many people. He had allowed his natural inclination toward sin to rule his life when he took another man's wife and had her husband murdered.

He came before God with deep sorrow, asking that he be given a new and cleansed heart, and for God to restore once again the joy of His salvation (vs. 12). We may never commit the terrible sins that David did, but each of us sins and stands with a heart in need of God's forgiveness and cleansing.

When the word "heart" is used in Scripture, it usually does not mean the organ in our chests that pumps our blood. It means the seat of our emotions, passions, appetites, intellect, morals, will, thoughts, spirit—the center and totality of our being—our very nature. Notice that David asks God to "create" a pure heart in him, which implies a new replacement heart, not just the patching up of an old defective one—making everything about him new and pure. Forgiving, renewing, and reforming the human heart/personality is one of God's greatest creative miracles.

David's great concern is to get his corrupt nature changed by a newly created heart with new thoughts, desires, motives, and purpose. He knew he could not change his heart in his own strength, and therefore pleads with God, the only One who can create, to create in him a clean/pure heart. The Hebrew word for "create" is the same word used to describe God's creation in Genesis 1:1. Speaking of God's creation, I'm reminded of 2 Corinthians 5:17: *". . . if anyone is in Christ, he is a new creation; The old is gone, the new has come!"*

When David asked God to renew a steadfast and right spirit within him, he was saying, "Lord, fix me for the future so that I will never depart from You and sin against You like this again." Each of us would do well to pray this same prayer.

Because he repented, God mercifully forgave David. If we repent, He will forgive us as well. *"If we confess our sins, he is faithful and just and will forgive us our sins and purify us from all unrighteousness"* (1 John 1:9 NIV).

Aug 03

Chuckle: Child's prayer: *"Dear God, maybe Cain and Abel would not kill each other so much if they each had their own rooms. It works out OK with me and my brother."*

Quote: *"Heaven is the most beautiful place the mind of God could conceive and the hand of God could create."* ~ R.G. Lee

Heavenly Promise

"Do not let your hearts be troubled. Trust (believe) in God; trust (believe) also in me. In my Father's house (heaven) are many (rooms) mansions; if it were not so, I would have told you. I am going there to prepare a place for you. And if I go and prepare a place for you, I will come back and take you to be with me that you also may be where I am" (John 14:1-4 NIV).

In our passage, Jesus' crucifixion was near. And I'm sure the disciples were beside themselves with fear, anxiety, and worry. They were about to lose their leader, mentor, teacher, and companion who had been with them constantly for the better part of three years. They had come to depend upon Him in so many ways. In His tender "Jesus" way, our Lord comforted His disciples with one of the most beautiful promises in the New Testament.

Each of us will experience death at a time of God's choosing. Also, each of us has, or will, experience the loss of someone very dear to us. It is a horrible experience when we lose a loved one. But I'm sure you will join me in thanking God that He has given each of us the capacity to grieve such losses.

We are created in the image of God and our ability to grieve reminds me of how God must grieve when He loses a precious soul who has rejected His love and the atoning blood of Jesus for the remission of sins—one who has said "no" to the promise of salvation and eternal life with God in a place the Bible calls heaven.

For those of us who have trusted Jesus as our Lord and Savior, we need not fear the time when our eternal souls leave our physical bodies. And as we grieve for other Christians we have lost, we should not grieve as those with no hope of seeing them again. Paul puts in this way: *"Brothers, we do not want you to be ignorant about those who fall asleep (die), or to grieve like the rest of men who have no hope"* (1 Thessalonians 4:13 NIV).

This brings us back to our passage from John. Jesus—right now—is preparing a place for each and every Christian. Dr. Paul Powell points out from Jesus' own words we are reminded that we have faith in the PERSON of Jesus Christ. *"Trust in God; trust also in me."* We also have faith in a PLACE in heaven that Jesus is preparing for us. *"I am going there to prepare a place for you."* Finally, we have faith in a PROMISE that Jesus will return and receive us into His presence so *"that we also may be where He is."*

If we have this kind of faith, it will ease the anxiety about our own deaths and make us realize that *"... to be absent from the body, and to be present with the Lord"* (2 Corinthians 5:8 NIV).

Praise Him for this Amazing Promise!!

Aug 04

Chuckle: *A Sunday School teacher asked little Johnny if he said prayers before eating?*

"No Sir," he replied. "We don't have to. My mom is a good cook!"

Quote: *"For God hath made you able to create worlds in your own mind which are more precious to Him than those which He created."* ~ Thomas Traherne

The Power of Imagination

"Now to him who is able to do immeasurably more than all we ask or imagine, according to his power that is at work within us, to him be glory in the church and in Christ Jesus throughout all generations . . ." (Ephesians 3:20-21 NIV).

Dotse and I are blessed with two wonderful children who make us very proud. When our firstborn daughter was two years old, I left home for a year-long tour of duty in Korea, and I returned when she was three. In my absence, our precious little girl had conjured up in her mind two imaginary friends and playmates named Patsy and Cory. I was amazed by how real her imaginary friends were to her. When we would go into the house or get into the car, she reminded us to hold the door open for Patsy and Cory.

As I think about those precious memories, I can't help but be amazed by the power of imagination, which can bring us great pleasure or great pain as we deal with imaginary people, things, or events.

Imagination is a powerful God-given human trait that adds great joy and excitement to our lives. Almost everything we do is influenced by our imagination. The creation of drama, poetry, or music that enriches our lives is inspired by imagination shaped by life's experiences. Imagination allows us to live in the world of make-believe. This is especially true for children. We can only conclude that when God created us, He did not overlook the value of imagination. Since God knew we could not see Him with our physical eyes, just maybe He gave us the ability to see Him through the eyes of our imagination.

By faith we can be *"certain of what we do not see"* (Hebrews 11:1 NIV). Our imagination helps us appreciate the fullness of that certainty. In our passage, Paul reminds us, however, that even our imagination is inadequate for accurately visualizing the attributes of God. He operates in a realm far beyond even our imagination.

Imagination can bring us unbelievable wonder, mystery, beauty, and joy. But there is also a dark side to our imagination. Runaway imagination may make you fear that the worst will happen, and your own thoughts may actually help bring it about. Someone has said, "Fear is the wrong use of imagination." We know many imaginary adversities we worry and fret about never materialize. Unjustified dread and fear can result in stress and anxiety that make us miserable and can even damage our health.

When we allow God to train and control our imaginations through our faith, we will begin to experience the abundant life that Jesus promised in John 10:10. As Christians, we need to capture, or recapture, the power of imagination as it is influenced by our unshakable faith in the One who gave us this wonderful gift— IMAGINATION!

Chuckle: *"If people were not meant to have late-night snacks, why is there a light in the refrigerator?"*

Quote: *"A miracle is an event which creates faith. Frauds deceive. An event which creates faith does not deceive; therefore it is not a fraud, but a miracle."* ~ George Bernard Shaw

The Impossible

"How will this be," Mary asked the angel, "since I am a virgin?" The angel answered, "The Holy Spirit will come upon you, and the power of the Most High will over-shadow you. So the holy one to be born will be called the Son of God. Even Elizabeth your relative is going to have a child in her old age, and she who was said to be barren is in her sixth month. For nothing is impossible with God" (Luke 1:34-37 NIV).

Just take a moment and let the significance of these words sink into your mind and heart. Here we see two women who were used of God—one to bring the Christ-child into our world and the other to birth John the Baptist who would herald Jesus' coming. Not in our wildest imagination could such a scenario of miraculous events be conceived. Miracles, by their very nature, are supernatural and originate from the realm of the "impossible." They baffle the minds of us mere humans. As acts of God, they seem to go against the known laws of nature, science, and reason. But some miracles seem even more impossible than others. Jesus said, *"What is impossible with men is possible with God"* (Luke 18:27 NIV).

God sent His Son into the world as a fulfilment of His promises to His people as written by the prophets. That same Jesus has made some wonderful promises to you and me. He has promised to give us eternal life through faith in Him. He has promised that our sins have been forgiven through His atoning death on the cross. He has promised that His Holy Spirit will live within us as believers to teach us, guide us, convict us, and encourage us. He has promised never to leave us or forsake us. He has promised to come back to earth a second time to claim His church and to take us into His presence for eternity. These are wonderful promises that, sadly, are seen as foolishness to many because they appear to be impossible and make no sense to carnal minds.

We can rejoice not only in celebration of Jesus' miraculous birth but for all He has done for us and for His promises for our future. It is by faith that we can claim these promises and have the complete assurance that what God says in His Word is absolutely true and reliable.

We know that God specializes in the impossible. If we understood everything about God, He wouldn't be God, but only an extension of our own minds. Let's rejoice that we serve a God who did the impossible by having a virgin conceive and be the Mother of our Lord Jesus Christ. If God can do this, He can certainly bring to reality the promises He has made to us—His children.

We can rejoice with Mary as she said, "... *the Mighty One has done great things for me—holy is his name*" (Luke 1:49 NIV).

Aug 06

Chuckle: *"Dates are for having fun, and people should use them to get to know each other. Even boys have something to say if you listen long enough."* ~ Lynnette, age 8

Quote: *"Rather than love, than money, than fame, give me truth."* ~ Henry David Thoreau

Itching Ears

"For the time will come when men will not put up with sound doctrine. Instead, to suit their own desires, they will gather around them a great number of teachers to say what their itching ears want to hear" (2 Timothy 4:3 NIV).

Have you ever made up your mind about something but were secretly bothered by doubt that you had made the right decision? Have you continued to ask people their opinions about it until you finally found someone who agreed with you? When you found someone who said what you wanted to hear, did that convince you that your decision was the right one? In our passage, we are warned that a time will come when people will no longer listen to the sound doctrinal truths of God's Word because they conflict with their worldly views and the lifestyles they have chosen.

Paul warns us about preachers and teachers who only teach what their audiences want to hear. I have seen people go from one church to another until they found a preacher who preached only that which made them feel good about themselves rather than convicting them of the disobedience and sin in their lives. I suppose every preacher has, at one time or another, been tempted to preach what the congregation wanted to hear rather than being faithful to God's Word and preaching what they needed to hear.

When you itch, it certainly feels good to have that itch scratched. But, as Christians, we should be thankful for preachers and teachers that refuse to scratch our itches. If you are a teacher, please don't sell your conscience in exchange for compliments from your audience. If you are a class or congregation member, do your ears itch to hear a certain opinion or do you thirst for the undiluted truth of God's Word?

Take, for example, the Biblical teaching that tithing a tenth of your income is God's standard. You may have made up your mind that you are not going to tithe, and you don't want to hear sermons on tithing because it makes you uncomfortable. Instead, you may want the preacher to be silent on the subject, or better yet, you want to be told it's alright for you to ignore God's instructions for His people. You need to have your itching ears scratched with justification for your position on the subject.

Let's pray together that each of us will long for the sound doctrinal truths from God's Word.

Someone has said, "The true function of preaching is to disturb the comfortable and to comfort the disturbed."

Aug 07

Chuckle: *TEACHER: "Winnie, name one important thing we have today that we didn't have ten years ago."*
WINNIE: "Me!"
Quote: *"Apart from Christ we know neither what our life nor our death is; we do not know what God is nor what we ourselves are."*
~ Blaise Pascal

Who Is Jesus Christ?

"But what about you?" he asked. "Who do you say I am?" Simon Peter answered, "You are the Christ, the Son of the living God" (Matthew 16:15-16 NIV).

You may be wondering why I would raise this question to my readers, most of whom are born again believers who have answered, to their own satisfaction, the question about the identity of Jesus Christ. Not only have they settled the issue of who Jesus is, but they are so sure of their conclusion that they have committed their lives to Him and placed their eternal souls in His hands—trusting His promise of eternity in heaven.

While Jesus was here on earth, there was much confusion about who He really was. Jesus asked His disciples what people were saying about His identity. *"Well" they replied, "some say John the Baptist, some say Elijah, and others say Jeremiah or one of the other prophets"* (vs. 14). It took Peter's enlightened answer for Jesus to say, *"Blessed are you, Simon son of Jonah, for this was not revealed to you by man, but by my Father in heaven"* (vs. 17). Faith like Peter's forms the foundation of God's kingdom.

Even today the identity of Jesus Christ is a matter of much disagreement. Some discount Him all together, while others acknowledge His importance in history because of His wise teachings. Many deny that He is God incarnate who lived on earth as a man and died to redeem mankind from enslavement to sin.

What would your answer be if Jesus were to ask you, *"Who*

do you say I am?"

Do you believe He was conceived by the Holy Spirit and born to the virgin Mary? *"The virgin will be with child and will give birth to a son, and they will call him Immanuel!—which means 'God with us'"* (Matthew 1:23).

Do you believe He, as God, came to earth as a human being to *"save his people from their sins?"* (Matthew 1:21).

Do you believe He suffered and died to pay the penalty for your sins and mine? *"While we were still sinners, Christ died for us"* (Romans 5:8).

Do you believe He rose again on the third day victorious over sin, death, and the grave? *"He is not here; he has risen, just as he said"* (Matthew 28:6).

Do you believe He is coming again someday to claim His church—all believers? *"So you also must be ready, because the Son of Man will come at an hour when you do not expect him"* (Matthew 24:44).

Do you believe that *"Salvation is found in no one else, for there is no other name under heaven given to men by which we must be saved?"* (Acts 4:12).

If you believe these truths and have a personal testimony concerning your own relationship with Jesus Christ, you should have no trouble answering Jesus' question, *"Who do you say I am?"*

Aug 08

Chuckle: Church Sign: *"God does not believe in atheists; therefore atheists do not exist!"*

Ponder This: *"The more a person loves, the closer he approaches the image of God."* ~ Unknown Author

Does Jesus Care About You?

"In all their suffering he also suffered, and he personally rescued them. In his love and mercy he redeemed them. He lifted them up and carried them through the years" (Isaiah 63:9 NLT).

Does our Lord really care what happens to me? Does He feel the pain that I feel? Can He understand what I'm going through? Yes, He does!

Because of His great love, God made provision to rescue us from the pain, sorrow, and eternal consequences of our sin. To do this, Jesus—the God man—came to earth as human. As a result He can empathize with us in every way.

Jesus fully understands our weaknesses and our fears. As our High Priest, He made Himself human, *"And because he is human, he is able to deal gently with the people, though they are ignorant and wayward. For he is subject to the same weaknesses we have"* (Hebrews 5:2 NLT). Since Jesus understands your pain, He pleads with you that you would be free from the suffering that sin causes, and He desires you to experience the peace, joy, and freedom that comes from a personal love relationship with Him.

Jesus is like us because He experienced a full range of temptations as a human being while here on earth. He faced temptations as we do—only more so. He is both sympathetic and empathetic toward us. We should be encouraged from knowing that Jesus faced temptation without giving in to sin. Through His example, and the power of the indwelling Holy Spirit, we can have the strength to resist sin and deal with hardships and suffering.

Jesus assures us of forgiveness and salvation. As humanity's representative, He is now at the right hand of the Father, interceding on our behalf. *"He lives forever to plead with God on our behalf"* (Hebrews 7:25 NLT). He is always available to hear us when we pray. *"And the Holy Spirit helps us in our distress. For we don't even know what we should pray for, nor how we should pray. But the Holy Spirit prays for us with groanings that cannot be expressed in words"* (Romans 8:26 NLT).

As we pray, the Holy Spirit penetrates to the deepest recesses of our being to help us root out those sinful thoughts and urges that we so carefully keep hidden from those around us. Aren't we foolish to think that there are some sins we can hide from God?

In the final analysis, our Lord really does understand what you are going through and is ready to help you. Through it all, our Lord remains our faithful companion and encourager because He identifies with us and understands what we are feeling.

This old hymn puts it this way: *"Just when I need Him, Jesus is near, Just when I falter, just when I fear; Ready to help me, ready to cheer. . . . Just when I need Him most."*

Aug 09

Chuckle: *"Light travels faster than sound. That's why some people appear bright until they speak."*

Quote: *"Humility is to make a right estimate of one's self."*
~ Charles Spurgeon

The Exalted Jesus

Therefore, God exalted him to the highest place and gave him the name that is above every name, that at the name of Jesus every knee should bow, in heaven and on earth and under the earth, and that every tongue confess that Jesus Christ is Lord, to the glory of God the Father" (Philippians 2:9-11a NIV).

"Therefore" in verse 9, seems to indicate that the Father's primary justification for exalting Jesus was because of His willingness to humble Himself and be obedient unto death on the cross. Through His humble service, Jesus pleased the Father, who made Him ruler of the universe. He was exalted to the highest place. He was given a name above every other name. And He was given the divine offices of Prophet, Jesus, Priest, Christ, and King. God wants every tongue to confess Jesus as Lord. Confession includes thanksgiving, praise, and commitment.

At the last judgment, even those who are condemned will recognize Jesus' authority and right to rule. People can choose now to commit their lives to Jesus as Lord or be forced to acknowledge Him as Lord when He returns. We are to lay up treasures in heaven by the way we live, love, and serve. Then, at the Judgment Seat of Christ (2 Cor. 5:10) we will receive the rewards for our faithful service. Jesus never sought to be exalted, but exaltation came as the result of His humble and obedient service. This should be our attitude.

The exalted Christ made this promise to those who have accepted Him as Savior and Lord. He said: *"I will come back and take you to be with me that you also may be where I am"* (John 14:3 NIV).

He could return at any moment. Are you ready to meet Him? If you are, how can you do anything less than praise Him as your Lord and humbly dedicate yourself to His service?

The following is attributed to Napoleon Bonaparte: *"I marvel that whereas the ambitious dreams of myself, Caesar, Alexander, should have vanished into thin air, a Judean peasant, Jesus, should be able to stretch His hands across the destinies of men and nations. I know men; and I tell you that Jesus Christ is no mere man. Between him and every other person in the world there is no possible term for comparison. Alexander, Caesar, Charlemagne, and I myself have founded empires; but upon what do these creations of our genius depend? Upon force. Jesus alone founded his empire upon love; and to this very day millions would die for him."*

Aug 10

Chuckle: *Have you heard about the bowlegged cowboy who was fired because he couldn't keep his calves together?*

Quote: *"Every Christian needs an half hour of prayer each day, except when he is busy, then he needs an hour."* ~ St Francis de Sales

Jesus' Model Prayer

"Our Father in heaven, may your name be honored. May your Kingdom come soon. May your will be done here on earth, just as it is in heaven. Give us our food for today, and forgive us our sins , just as we have forgiven those who have sinned against us. And don't let us yield to temptation, but deliver us from the evil one" (Matthew 6:9-12 NLT).

Jesus' words here are commonly called "The Lord's Prayer." But since Jesus was teaching His disciples how to pray, it could be called the "Model Prayer." Let's focus on both the sequence and content of the prayer.

First, we are to begin our prayer by honoring God as we enter His holy presence with praise, reverence, and commitment. *"Our Father in heaven, may your name be honored."* We focus our attention on the holiness and majesty of God and spend some time just sharing our love for Him. But it's tempting to skip this most important part of the prayer and go directly to our selfish shopping list of things we want God to do for us.

Second, we express our concerns for God's spiritual kingdom and His will. *"May Your Kingdom come soon. May your will be done here on earth, just as it is in heaven."* Our concern should be to glorify God and advance His kingdom above all else. Jesus said, *"And he, God, will give you all you need from day to day if you live for him and make the Kingdom of God your primary concern"* (Matthew 6:33 NLT). This means seeking His will first before making our personal requests. Our prayers should focus on the furtherance of God's kingdom as enunciated in the Great Commission (see Matthew 28:19-20).

Third, our prayer now turns to our daily needs from God, our sustainer and provider. *"Give us our food for today."* By now, our prayer is totally focused on God, not ourselves. We will have rearranged our priorities and affirmed our complete trust in God and His will. We now understand that if we put God and His kingdom first, He will provide everything else we may need. Selfishness has been removed from our prayer

Fourth, we acknowledge God's provision by asking His help in dealing with our daily struggles. *"Forgive us our sins, just as we have forgiven those who have sinned against us. And don't let us yield to temptation, but deliver us from the evil one."* Notice that God's forgiveness is requested based on our forgiveness of others. Also, we should ask God to give us strength to overcome temptation and lead us in His way instead.

We often reverse the order of the Model Prayer by first voicing our real and perceived needs and spend little, if any, time seeking God and His kingdom. Let's take a new look at the Model Prayer and bring our priorities in line with those modelled by Jesus.

Aug 11

Chuckle: *After a session with his parents, a little boy taped to his parents' door a note that read: "Dear parents, Be nice to your children and they will be nice to you. Love, God."*

Quote: *"He who provides for this life, but takes no care for eternity, is wise for the moment but a fool forever."*
~ Unknown Author

When Least Expected

"Now, brothers, about times and dates we do not need to write you, for you know very well that the day of the Lord will come like a thief in the night" (1 Thessalonians 5:1-2 NIV).

A major theme in New Testament Scriptures is the second coming of Jesus Christ. One of the clearest statements on the subject comes from the lips of Jesus Himself. *"And if I go to prepare a place for you, I will come back and take you to be with me that you may be where I am"* (John 14:3 NIV).

The promise of Jesus' return is a precious tenet of the Christian faith. Numerous passages attest to the fact that He will come again to "rapture" His church, which includes all those whose sins have been covered by His atoning blood sacrifice. He will take us to be with Him forever. You can read about how this will happen in 1 Thessalonians 4:13-18.

The promise—and our blessed hope—that Jesus will return has spawned numerous questions about when and how this will happen. People down through the ages have made all sorts of predictions and some have even set specific dates when Jesus would return—all have been proven wrong. Speculating about the date of Christ's return is wasted effort and foolish.

Listen to Jesus own words: *"No one knows about that day or hour, not even the angels in heaven, nor the Son, but only the Father. . . . Therefore keep watch, because you do not know on what day your Lord will come. . . . So you also must be ready, because the Son of Man will come at an hour when you do not expect him"* (Matthew 24:36, 42, 44 NIV).

Even though we do not know when Jesus will return, we are to live with the expectation that He could come at any moment. If you knew that Jesus' return was imminent, how would it change the way you live? Would it make a difference in your faithfulness to Him and in the way you serve other people? Would it cause you to fall on your knees and repent of your sins? Would it cause you to get your spiritual house in order in preparation for meeting your Lord? Look at Jesus' words again: *"So you also must be ready"* as if He were coming today.

Since the Lord will return suddenly and unexpectedly, my plea to you who do not know Him as Savior and Lord is that you give your heart and life to Him today—that you repent of your sins, ask His forgiveness, and commit your life to Him in faith.

If you are already a Christian, I encourage you to bring your life into line with God's standards for His followers and be ready to meet Him with confidence and joy and without fear.

Aug 12

Chuckle: *A blurb in a church bulletin read, "Ladies, don't forget the rummage sale. It's a chance to get rid of those things not worth keeping around the house. Don't forget your husbands....!"*
Question: *"What kind of a church would my church be if all its members were just like me?*

Copying Jesus Christ

"Be imitators of God, therefore as dearly loved children, and live a life of love, just as Christ loved us and gave himself for us as a fragrant offering and sacrifice to God" (Ephesians 5:1-2 NIV).

We often hear the term "role model" when describing someone whose life reflects the good qualities of character that we admire. I'm sure each of us has someone we look up to as a role model.

Having worthy human role models is good, but living with Jesus as your role model is best. If we pattern our lives after other humans, we become a copy of a copy, and imperfections and flaws have a way of creeping into copies of copies. It's much better to copy the original, thus we should seek to copy Jesus.

We are to live as God's children by imitating our heavenly Father. If you are a born again believer, you are a child of God by spiritual birth and have been given a new nature. You could say you have the spiritual DNA of God, and it's only logical that we should act like our Lord. If you heard a cat bark or a dog meow, you would know right away that something was amiss. Their outward appearance and actions should be consistent with their nature. If you are a child of God, you should act like it by living like Jesus in the power of the Holy Spirit, from whom your new nature is derived.

Just as children imitate their parents, we are instructed to imitate God, as His children, by living a life of love. Christ's great love for us caused Him to sacrifice Himself to give us new life and His nature. This kind of love for others goes far beyond affection and results in self-sacrificing acts of service. To live a life of love means that we are filled, saturated, and permeated by the same unconditional love that Christ demonstrated for us on the cross. As Jesus was hanging on that cross in agony, His love showed through with this prayer for those who were crucifying Him: *"Father, forgive them, for they do not know what they are doing"* (Luke 23:34 NIV).

This kind of love is not reciprocal—it is unconditional and makes no demands. It's the kind of love God showed as described in Romans 5:8 and 6:23. *"But God demonstrates his own love for us in this: While we were still sinners, Christ died for us." "For the wages of sin is death, but the gift of God is eternal life in Christ Jesus our Lord."*

To copy the love of Christ is to copy the love of God, the Father, because the Bible tells us they are one. We copy the love of Christ by loving others as He has loved us. Jesus said, *"A new command I give you: Love one another. As I have loved you, so you must love one another"* (John 13:34 NIV). This kind of love is shown when we share Christ with the lost people, and by even loving those who do not love us in return.

Aug 13

Chuckle: *What did Paul Revere say at the end of his famous ride? "Whoa."*

Quote: *"Faith is not belief without proof, but trust without reservations."* ~ Elton Trueblood

Faith That Triumphs

Jesus said, *"Simon, Simon, Satan has asked to have all of you, to sift you like wheat. But I have pleaded in prayer for you, Simon, that your faith should not fail. So when you have repented and turned to me again, strengthen and build up your brothers"* (Luke 22:32 NLT).

In wars like those in Iraq and Afghanistan, our troops often have difficulty identifying the enemy because they look no different than those on our side. It's not easy to know who your enemy is. The same is true with our greatest enemy, Satan, because he often disguises himself so as to appear friendly and harmless. In life as in war, our first major task is to identify the enemy. Our enemy wants to separate us from fellowship with our Lord and render us ineffective as ambassadors and witnesses for Him.

In our passage, Satan wanted to crush Simon Peter and Jesus' other followers like grains of wheat. It was his hope that nothing would be left of them except worthless chaff to be blown away. But Jesus encouraged Peter. Although his faith would falter, it would not be destroyed. It would return stronger than ever and Peter would become a strong and effective leader.

You may be going through a time when your faith is faltering. Your enemy may have enticed you away and you may not be walking as closely with your Lord as you once did. Perhaps you feel ineffective as a testimony to others. If these conditions apply to you, rest assured Satan is the responsible culprit.

The first thing you must do is identify your enemy. To do this it's important that you remember three things about Satan:

- He is real and active.

- He is your enemy and he is on the attack.
- His power is limited by what God allows. He asked permission to sift Peter.

Once you have identified your enemy, you must rely on your Lord as your advocate. In verse 32, Jesus showed His advocacy for Peter by telling Peter He was praying for him. Peter's faith faltered when he denied his lord three times, as Jesus predicted in verse 34, but he rebounded and ultimately did not fail.

Please remember that Jesus is praying for you. Listen: *"Therefore he (Jesus) is able, once and forever, to save everyone who comes to God through him. He lives forever to plead with God on their behalf"* (Hebrews 7:25 NLT). Also, be aware that the Holy Spirit lives within you to give you strength (see John 14:16). *"Submit yourselves to God. Resist the devil and he will flee from you"* (James 4:7 NIV).

Whenever Satan knocks, let Jesus answer the door. You will then experience triumphant faith which will also strengthen your brothers and sisters in Christ.

Chuckle: *A drill sergeant had chewed out a young cadet, and as he walked away, he said to the cadet, "I guess when I die you'll come and dance on my grave."*

The cadet replied, "Not me, Sarge! I promised myself that when I got out of the Army, I'd never stand in another line."

Quote: *"Fear is never a good counselor and victory over fear is the first spiritual duty of man."* ~ Nicolas Berdyaev

Fear Can Be a Prison

"And because of my imprisonment, many of the Christians here have gained confidence and become more bold in telling others about Christ" (Philippians 1:14 NLT).

I read about a woman who never shared her faith at work because she feared repercussions from her superiors and possible rejection by her own workmates. She was even afraid she would lose her job. She was encouraged by a friend to entrust her fear to the Holy Spirit and be bold in sharing the love of Christ with others. She did so, and in her case, there were no negative consequences as she had feared.

In our passage, Paul was in prison in Rome and his boldness to proclaim the gospel, even while in chains, served as encouragement to others. Paul saw his circumstances as an opportunity to spread the good news of Christ. He looked for ways to demonstrate his faith even in the most difficult of times. Because of his boldness, Roman soldiers of the palace guard heard the gospel, as well as other Christians, and they were encouraged to put aside their fears of persecution and be faithful witnesses for Christ.

Fear of being rejected or persecuted is a major factor in the failure of many Christians to share their faith. I dare say we have all experienced such fear at some point. Fear can become a prison far stronger than the chains that held Paul. Fear can literally paralyze and prevent us from doing anything for our Lord. If you are imprisoned by fear when it comes to sharing your Christian testimony, you are depending upon your own strength rather than the power of the Holy Spirit. Christ Himself will unlock the doors of your prison of fear and give you the bold words He wants you to say if you are willing to trust Him.

Another important deterrent to your fear is the strong conviction that God has given you a message to deliver that your audience desperately needs to hear. Such a conviction will help free us from our prison of fear. When commanded by Jewish religious leaders not to speak or teach in the name of Jesus or face punishment, Peter and John replied, *". . . we cannot help speaking about what we have seen and heard"* (Acts 4:20 NIV). Later they prayed, *"Now, Lord consider their threats and enable your servants to speak your word with great boldness"* (Acts 4:29 NIV).

Let's pray together that our fear will not imprison us and we will be courageous enough to speak fearlessly in the power of the Holy Spirit.

Aug 15

Chuckle: *A teenager complained to a friend: "My dad wants me to have all the things he never had as a boy—including straight A's on my report card."*

Quote: *"We must become acquainted with our emotional household; we must see our feelings as they actually are, not as we assume they are. This breaks their hypnotic and damaging hold on us."* ~ Vernon Howard

Feelings Are Unreliable

"Therefore, prepare your minds for action; be self-controlled; set your hope fully on the grace to be given you when Jesus Christ is revealed. As obedient children do not conform to the evil desires (feelings) you had when you lived in ignorance. But just as he who called you is holy, so be holy in all you do" (1 Peter 1:13-15 NIV).

In my military pilot training, I was taught to fly aircraft by instruments. When flying in clouds, and other conditions of low visibility, it becomes necessary to fly solely from the information displayed on the aircraft's instruments. One of the most difficult things to learn is how to ignore your feelings when you have no visual reference to the ground—or horizon—and believe what the instruments are telling you. Trying to fly based on feelings can lead to disaster as vertigo sets in. Your feelings are totally unreliable, and the factual information being displayed by the instruments must be trusted for safe flight.

Do you make life's decisions based on feelings? Do you attend church only when you feel like it? Do you live your life by moods and emotions? Either your feelings master you, or you master your feelings. Don't get me wrong, emotions and feelings are God-given and are very important for a happy life. The problem is, our feelings can misdirect us.

Here are three true or false statements—I should live my life: (1) based on my feelings; (2) based on my faith; or (3) or based on facts.

If we live by our feelings, we will make many mistakes because they are unreliable. Therefore, this statement is false.

Whether or not we should live by faith depends on the object of that faith—not faith in self, some philosophy, new age concept, or some person who is unreliable. Unless faith is in Christ, this statement is also false.

It's true, we should live based on facts—the facts of God's Word. Jesus said *"You shall know the truth and the truth shall set you free"* (John 8:32 NIV). God's Word is true whether I believe it or not—whether I act upon it or not—whether I feel good about it or not.

Bill Bright used a Train Diagram to put our feelings in perspective. The Engine represents the facts of God's Word. The Coal Car is faith which provides the fuel. And the Caboose represents feelings. You cannot drive the train from the caboose. Believing God's Word and acting on it is the key.

Like the aircraft instruments, God's Word always has an accurate and reliable message for me when my feelings get in the way of His will for my life. If we are to win at Life, we must be good students of the Scriptures and make life's decisions based their truths—not how we feel.

Aug 16

Chuckle: *"Cosmetics were used in the Middle Ages; in fact they're still used in the middle ages."*

Quote: *"You cannot make yourself feel something you do not feel, but you can make yourself do right in spite of your feelings."* ~ Pearl S. Buck

Feelings and God's Will

"Do not conform yourselves any longer to the pattern of this world, but be transformed by the renewing of your mind. Then you will be able to test and approve what God's will is—his good, pleasing and perfect will" (Romans 12:2 NIV).

Our feelings are not reliable and often mislead us. Here are some examples:

- Sometimes Christians may feel worthless to God and others. This may be the way you feel, but God sees you as His precious child, a citizen of heaven, a special person.
- You may not feel God's presence in your life. Does this mean His presence is not with you? When you feel this way, read Hebrews 13:5, *"Never will I leave you; never will I forsake you."* This promise is true regardless of our feelings.
- Sometimes we don't feel the strength to do what we know God wants us to do. Remember, *"I can do all things through Christ who gives me strength"* (Philippians 4:13 NIV)—if I trust Him and not my feelings.

Feelings are influenced by circumstances, people, and the devil. We must test our feelings against the truths of His Word. Satan will try to get you to doubt divine truths and make you feel down and discouraged. Feelings must not be allowed to determine your decisions in life. Your feelings of need for acceptance, approval, belonging, etc., may mislead you into making bad decisions that can ruin your life.

If you purchase your dream home based on your feelings and it is beyond your means, trouble is on the way. Your decision was not based on truth.

The most basic truth is, if you don't accept Jesus Christ as Savior, you will spend eternity separated from God in a place the Bible calls "hell"—no matter how you feel about it.

Can you see the problem with making important decisions based on feelings? Controlling our feelings is not easy. This quote reveals the reason:

"The human personality is said to consist of roughly four-fifths emotions and one-fifth intellect. This means that our decisions are arrived at on the basis of 80 percent emotions and feelings, and only 20 percent intellect and reasoning. To engage in a confrontation, or even a discussion, without taking emotions into account is to be only 20 percent effective in your dealings with people." ~ Unknown Source

Understanding the importance of human emotions is essential for successful interpersonal relationships. We must also recognize how powerful our own emotions and feelings are and let God's will from His Word override our feelings when it comes to making life's decisions.

Aug 17

Chuckle: *TEACHER: "Clyde, your composition on 'My Dog' is exactly the same as your brother's. Did you copy his?"*
CLYDE: "No, teacher, it's the same dog."
Quote: *"When we have 'second thoughts' about something, our first thoughts don't seem like thoughts at all—just feelings."*
~ Sydney J. Harris

Feelings in Perspective

"Surely you heard of Christ and were taught in Him in accordance with the truth that is in Jesus. You were taught with regard to your former way of life, to put off your old self, which is being corrupted by its deceitful desires, feelings; to be made new in the attitude of your minds; and to put on the new self, created to be like God in true righteousness and holiness" (Ephesians 4:21-22 NIV).

The proper order for making life's decisions is facts, faith, and finally, feelings. *"Take a strong foundation, build a house upon it, and then above the house you have the clouds and the weather. The foundation is the fact/truth of God's Word; the house is our faith settled down on the foundation; the weather represents our feelings because it is constantly changing—coming and going."* ~ Unknown Source.

Let's consider the following two truths:

1. *I should make the right decision, take the right action, and do the right things based on God's truth, not how I feel.* The Bible says we are to renew our minds. How does God renew our minds? Through His Word—His truth. God wants us to choose to do the right thing even before we feel like it. If you wait until you feel like reading your Bible, praying, attending church, witnessing, doing the right thing, you won't do much—that is until God matures you to the point that your desires and feelings begin to correspond with His truth. His Spirit will empower you to choose to do what's right.

Paul said we should put off the old way of thinking by

saturating ourselves with divine truth, then living it—even when we don't feel like it.

2. *I should constantly affirm the truth of God's Word.* We are to *prepare our minds for action and be self-controlled.* How do you do this? You choose to do what God says in His Holy Word. As you affirm the truths of God's Word, you can make decisions and take actions you never thought you could make or do. *"I can do all things through Christ who strengthens me"* (Philippians 4:13).

If you have feelings of doubt and insecurity, listen:

"This then is how we know we belong to the truth, and how we set our hearts at rest in his presence whenever our hearts condemn us. For God is greater than our hearts and he knows everything" (1 John 3:19-20 NIV).

If I confess my sins and ask God to empower me, then He will give me strength. To win at life, we must learn to control the way we feel. Remember, God is in control even when you feel nothing. We must rely on His promises and His truth. True Christian maturity comes when our feelings begin to correspond, through faith, with His truth and will. *"Your attitude should be the same as that of Christ Jesus"* (Philippians 2:5 NIV).

Aug 18

Chuckle: *TV repairman: "So, what seems to be the problem with your TV?"*
Woman: *"It has double images. I hope you men can fix it."*
Quote: *"No conceivable life can be so interesting and stimulating as that which we live in Christ."* ~ William Little

Finding Your Life

Jesus said, *"If you cling to your life, you will lose it; but if you give up your life for me, you will find it"* (Matthew 10:39 NLT).

To the unsaved, and even to immature Christians, these words from Jesus are difficult to understand. It's a great paradox that one finds his life by being willing to lose it, just as he inevitably loses his life by trying to save it. The contrast is between living selfishly only for ourselves, and living sacrificially for Christ. Each person can find eternal life, and the abundant life here on earth, by surrendering his or her life to Christ, or forfeit it by indulging in self-trust, self-love, and self-assertion.

It's believed that Jesus may have also been making a reference to martyrdom. The one who, under trial, seemingly saves his life by renouncing Christ actually loses it; but the one who remains faithful suffers martyrdom for acknowledging his faith in Christ. He seems to have lost his life but actually finds his life in Christ.

What is the practical application of Jesus' words for us as we live each day? Simply stated, we must get our priorities in the right order. We can become so busy and preoccupied with our own lives that our priorities become upside down. The least important becomes most important. The most important becomes least important. The valueless becomes most valuable and the most valuable becomes a mere trinket in our flawed value systems.

The more we love the things of this world (leisure, power, popularity, wealth), the more we discover how relatively unimportant they are in God's grand scheme of things. The life Christ wants for us can only be achieved by loosening our greedy grasp on earthly rewards and follow Christ with His eternal rewards. Then we will understand and claim the promises of our Lord when He said, *"I have come that they (we) may have life and have it to the full"* (John 10:10 NIV).

Our Lord wants our lives to be abundantly full and rich in Him, both here on earth and in eternity. Our eternal lives begin the moment we pray to receive Him as personal Lord and Savior. Have you claimed Christ's offer in your life? Are you living for Christ or for yourself?

Aug 19

Chuckle: *Mom shouted to her young son, "Be careful, I just waxed the floor."*

Jimmy said, "Don't worry, Mom, I'm wearing cleats."

Quote: *"Never does the human soul appear so strong and noble as when it foregoes revenge and dares to forgive an injury."*
~ E. H. Chapin

Forgiveness: Unconditional Grace

"But if you do not forgive, neither will your Father Who is in heaven forgive your transgressions" (Mark 11:26 NIV). *"For if you forgive others for their transgressions, your heavenly Father will also forgive you"* (Matthew 6:14 NIV). *"Be kind and compassionate to one another, forgiving each other, just as, in Christ, God forgave you"* (Ephesians 4:32 NIV).

In the New Testament four Greek words are used in dealing with "forgiveness." They mean: to deal graciously with, to dispatch or send away, to release, and to overlook. If we digest these meanings, we can better understand the Psalmist when he says God's forgiveness *"removes our sins as far as the east is from the west."* Our sins are remembered no more—as if they never occurred.

Forgiveness is a word of such unconditional grace that its true meaning often challenges each of us to go beyond where we are willing to go, to reconcile with our brother or sister. In the New Testament several points are made clear. First, the forgiven sinner must forgive others. *"Forgive and you will be forgiven"* (Luke 6:37). Second, forgiveness is to be whole-hearted and complete. It is to be like Christ's forgiveness. *"Forgive as the Lord forgave you"* (Colossians 3:13).

Have you ever been so consumed by anger or felt such severe pain that you wanted to withhold forgiveness until your offender begged for it? Do we demand that the offender grovel at our feet in apology—sometimes over and over again?

By making our forgiveness so dependent on the actions of the offender, we grant considerable power over our lives to the one who injured us—setting us up to be a victim twice!

Thus we continue to harbor anger, which we allow to fester and rob us of our joy as Christians. We should never allow the actions of another person to deprive us of the joy and contentment that our faith in Jesus Christ has brought to us. Simply stated, if you enjoy eternal forgiveness from God, you need to be willing to forgive others here in the present, which is an act of unconditional grace.

Let's not allow the actions of others to become a stumbling block in our walk with our Lord. We have been forgiven much, and in the same way, we must forgive others and release to the Lord those who've hurt us. He has promised that He will repay, if payment is due, and God keeps His word. *"Shall not the Judge of all the earth do right?"* (Genesis 18:25).

By releasing our offender, we truly set ourselves free! By graciously forgiving those who offend you, and letting them know of that forgiveness, you serve as an inspiration to them and others. As you model Biblical forgiveness, you become useful in God's hands to impact the lives of others.

Aug 20

Chuckle: *"I write down everything I want to remember. That way, instead of spending a lot of time trying to remember what it is I wrote down, I spend the time looking for the paper I wrote it down on."* ~ Beryl Pfizer

Quote: *"We are silent at the beginning of the day because God should have the first word, and we are silent before going to sleep because the last word also belongs to God."* ~ Dietrich Bonnhoeffer

When God Seems Far Away

"I can never escape from your Spirit! I can never get away from your presence!" (Psalm 139:7 NLT).

There are times in our lives when God seems far away and unreachable. It seems as if He has left us all alone. When you feel this way, it is time to do two things.

First, examine your heart. Is there is sin in your life? Have you truly been seeking God through faithful obedience?

Second, trust God's promises, not your feelings.

God's Word is replete with assurances of God's presence with believers at all times. God has said, *"Never will I leave you; never will I forsake you"* (Hebrews 13:5b NIV). *"And surely I am with you always, to the very end of the age"* (Matthew 28:20b NIV). These are solemn promises from our Lord Himself—never will He abandon us—never will He break His promises. How is Jesus with us?

He was with His disciples physically until He ascended into heaven and then through His Holy Spirit. He promised that the Holy Spirit would be His presence that would never leave them—or us. *"And I will ask the Father, and he will give you another Counselor, Holy Spirit, who will never leave you"* (John 14:16 NLT). This promise is to each of us if we have been born again.

If you need further assurance of God's never-ending presence in your life, listen again to the psalmist: *"You both precede and follow me. You place your hand of blessing on my head. . . . I can* never escape from your Spirit! I can never get away from your presence" (Psalm 137:5, 7 NLT). God is always with you, and absolutely nothing can ever separate you from His love. "I know the Lord is always with me. I will not be shaken, for he is right beside me" (Psalm 16:8 NLT). You can take these truths to the bank. When you feel like God is far away from you, claim these promises.

God's Word tells us that our lives are temples of the Holy Spirit because the Spirit of Christ lives within us. However, it would be wrong to assume by this that our lives are always pleasing to Him. Instead, we must prepare our hearts so that God will choose to reveal His presence to us. "Draw close to God and he will draw close to you." If you're not sensing God's presence, go to Him in prayer and ask for the faith to experience Him once again. Faith is unconditional trust even when you feel that God is far away.

I'm reminded of a little story about a man and wife who were riding in their pickup truck. The wife asked the husband who was driving, "Why don't we sit close together like we did when we were younger?" The man replied, "I haven't moved."

God does not move away from us. If you feel He is far away, you have moved away from Him.

Aug 21

Chuckle: *Michelangelo's mother: "Can't you paint on walls like other children? Do you have any idea how hard it is to get that stuff off the ceiling?"*

Quote: *"Show me the way, Not to fortune and fame, Not how to win Laurels Or praise for my name—But show me the way To spread 'The Great Story' That Thine is The Kingdom And Power and Glory."*
~ Helen Steiner Rice

God's Call on Your Life

"Then I heard the voice of the Lord saying, 'Whom shall I send? And who will go for us?' And I said, 'Here am I. Send me!" (Isaiah 6:8 NIV).

This powerful passage reminds us that God calls His people for specific purposes. It also reminds us that the response which pleases and honors God is "Here I am, send me." Or "Here I am Lord and I will gladly do whatever you wish me to do."

God's call is not only for a select few, but for every believer. Isaiah was listening to a non-specific call from God when he personalized it by stepping forward in complete abandon to make himself available for whatever God had in store for him. Whether we hear God's call depends on the condition of our hearts and spiritual ears. And how we interpret that call depends on our spiritual mindset. Am I listening for the call of God? Will I hear Him when He calls? Or, am I so far away from God that I can't hear His voice?

"But if thine heart turn away, so that thou wilt not hear (and obey), but shalt be drawn away, and worship other God's and serve them; I denounce (declare) unto you this day, that ye shall surely perish. . ." (Deuteronomy 30:17-18 KJV).

We see here the classic pattern of people drifting away and rebelling against God. You see, if our hearts are turned away from God, we will not hear Him. Then we will establish other substitute gods in our lives—anything that becomes more important to us than our relationship and fellowship with God. When this process has run its course, we will no longer be listening for the call of the One True God. We will not hear the still, small voice of invitation to join Him in fulfilling His purpose for our lives.

As a pastor, I have had Christians say they did not sense God calling them to teach a Bible study class, serve on a committee, or to witness to a lost friend. Sometimes our hearts can turn away from God and toward other things. Then we can move so far from God that we are unable to hear His call and don't know if God is calling us or not. We may not be listening for God's call because our hearts are turned away to other selfish things.

To hear God's call, we must listen intently and with purpose.

Aug 22

Chuckle: *A patient said to his dentist, "Doctor, I have yellow teeth, what do I do?"*

The dentist replied, "Wear a brown tie!"

Quote: *"Materialism has nothing to do with amount, it has everything to do with attitude"* ~ Unknown Author

Things That Last

"Since you have been raised to new life with Christ, set your sights on the realities of heaven, where Christ sits at God's right hand in the place of honor and power" (Colossians 3:1 NLT). *"But store up for yourselves treasures in heaven, where moth and rust do not destroy, and where thieves do not break in and steal"* (Matthew 6:20 NIV).

I'm always getting solicitations in the mail wanting me to purchase extended warranties on everything from our cars to household appliances. Such warranties are designed to protect us from the inevitable failures of the things we buy. They help give us peace of mind about the "what ifs" in life. Material things cannot be expected to last forever, although many seem to think they will. Without faith, it's much easier to focus on the things we can see and touch here on earth rather than the unseen things above.

No extended warranty is needed in your relationship with your Lord. The salvation we enjoy in Christ is complete and will never fail us or need repair or overhaul. Nothing in addition to what Christ did on the cross is ever needed. *". . . nor anything in all creation, will be able to separate us from the love of God that is in Christ Jesus"* (Romans 8:19 NIV). When God designed our salvation, He intended it to last forever and to give us peace of mind and faith that our eternal destiny is secure in Him.

Our challenge is to think about things above and not be enamored with material things on earth. This is extremely difficult unless our focus remains on the eternal rather than the temporary.

Setting our sights on heaven will help us put heavenly priorities into daily practice here and now. We do this by concentrating on acts of obedience to God. It includes *". . . seeking first his kingdom and his righteousness, and all these (material) things will be given to you as well"* (Matthew 6:33 NIV).

What is most important to you? Is it the material things you have and the need for extended warranties to make them last? Our material things can easily push God out of our lives and cause our concern for the eternal to fade into the background. If we seek things of eternal value, we will continually look forward to the day when we will meet Christ face-to-face.

Aug 23

Chuckle: *A father was reading Bible stories to his young son. He read, "The man named Lot was warned to take his wife and flee out of the city, but his wife looked back and was turned into a pillar of salt."*

His son asked, "What happened to the flea?"

Quote: *"My great concern is not whether God is on our side, my great concern is to be on God's side."* ~ Abraham Lincoln

Boasting in the Lord

"The person who wishes to boast should boast only of what the Lord has done" (1 Corinthians 1:31 NLT).

Many of us like to draw attention to ourselves by boasting about what we have done. Some have the idea that the way to earn God's favor and attain eternal life is to live a moral life. If we can convince God of our "goodness," surely He will find us acceptable in His sight. But we must realize that skills, wisdom, and good deeds do not get a person into God's kingdom—simple faith in Jesus Christ does. Let's delve into this amazing truth more deeply and learn how to satisfy our desire to boast.

In our passage, Paul gives us some sage advice concerning boasting. It's easy for us to want the credit for all the good things in life as if we had earned them all on our own. When we begin to think too highly of ourselves, we risk having our pride take control and everything becomes about us and what we have done. *"Do not think of yourself more highly than you ought, but rather think of yourself with sober judgment, in accordance with the measure of faith God has given you"* (Romans 12:3 NIV). We are warned that *"Pride goes before destruction, a haughty spirit before a fall"* (Proverbs 16:18 NIV).

Our pride and boasting should always be about what God has done. That way He receives all the honor He deserves. When it comes to our salvation, no one can boast that personal achievements helped him or her secure eternal life. Our salvation is a gift from God through our faith in Jesus Christ. We can never be "good" enough to earn it. *"For it is by grace you have been saved, through faith—and this not from yourselves, it is a gift of God—not by works, so that no one can boast"* (Ephesians 2:8-9 NIV).

If we have been saved by God's grace through faith, what is the significance of doing good deeds/works? This verse reveals the answer: *"For we are God's workmanship, created in Christ Jesus to do good works, which God prepared in advance for us to do"* (Ephesians 2:10 NIV). Our good works are to glorify God, not to earn our way into His favor.

If we recognize that everything we are and everything we have comes from God, we have accepted the truth that *"Every good and perfect gift is from above, coming down from the Father . . ."* (James 1:17 NIV). When we glorify God, we praise Him and our only boasting is about what He has done in our lives.

Aug 24

Chuckle: *A child prayed, "Dear God, Thank you for the baby brother but I asked for a puppy. I never asked for anything before. You can look it up." Joyce*

Quote: *"As we learn to shorten the time between offense and forgiveness, there becomes no time left for anger or vindictiveness."* ~ Unknown Source

Condemning Other Christians

"So why do you condemn another Christian? Why do you look down on another believer? Remember, each of us will stand personally before the judgment seat of God... Yes, each of us will give a personal account to God. So don't condemn each other anymore. Decide instead to live in such a way that you will not put an obstacle in another Christian's path" (Romans 14:10,12-13 NLT).

As we study the history of the Christian faith and church, we find numerous incidences where spiritual pride was the basis for criticism of fellow believers. There are some Christian practices that the Bible leaves open to interpretation, and these differences of interpretation often become major sources of disagreement and conflict.

In Romans, chapter 14, Paul deals with this issue. His thesis is that in Christian practice where there is room for interpretation, we are to accept one another in love even when we disagree

I know many Christians who practice some aspects of their faith and worship differently than I do, but this makes them no less faithful to their Lord. If a person has been saved by God's grace through faith in Jesus Christ, and Him alone, as Savior and Lord and is committed to serving Him, the principle requirement of faith has been fulfilled. We should always be considerate, encouraging, and accepting of other Christians rather than being critical, condescending, and condemning.

The church must stand fast against practices that are expressly forbidden in God's Word. But they should not create additional rules and regulations and make them as important as God's specific instructions. Too often believers base their judgments of others on personal opinion, preference, or adherence to tradition. By doing so, our own lack of faith is exposed in that we don't think God can guide His children without our help.

Paul's message is that we should remain strong in our faith while being sensitive to the faith of others. When we consider the feelings of others before our own, we will always be amazed at the response we will receive. It is very difficult for people to return unkindness when they become convinced they are loved and appreciated—when they know their best interests are a major consideration in a relationship.

None of us is so strong in our faith that we are without weaknesses. We should always be concerned about the effects of our behavior on others. As we grow in our faith, we will become more concerned about giving an account to God for our own actions rather than judging those of others.

Aug 25

Chuckle: *"A pastor resigned from one church because of health and exhaustion . . . They were sick and tired of him!"*

Quote: *"Contentment is a pearl of great price, and whoever procures it at the expense of ten thousand desires makes a wise and a happy purchase."* ~ Balguy

The Secret of Being Content

". . . . for I have learned to be content whatever the circumstances. . . . I have learned the secret of being content in any and every situation, whether well fed or hungry, whether living in plenty or in want. I can do everything through him who gives me strength" (Philippians 4:11-12 NIV).

Two little teardrops were floating down the river of life. One asked, "Who are you?" "I'm a teardrop from a girl who loved a man and lost him. But who are you?" The first teardrop replied, "I'm a teardrop from the girl who got him!"

Life is like that. We cry for things we can't have, but we might cry twice as hard if we had received them. Jesus spoke often of qualities that produce peace and contentment. Do you know individuals you would classify as content? Are you content with your life? Do others think of you when they name contented people?

I believe it is a greater challenge to be content while having much and using it properly with a Christ-like spirit, than it is while having little. Often it seems that the more we have, the more we want—never quite satisfied or content. Notice that Paul said, *"I have learned the secret of being content."* Contentment is not a trait that is obtained naturally—it is a supernatural condition available for Christians who have learned its secret.

Learning to be content is a process which takes time. You can't expect to master skiing or golf the first time you try. You must learn. Paul said he had learned to be content even while in prison chains. His contentment did not depend on external circumstances.

He noted the terrible circumstances in which he learned contentment in 2 Corinthians 11:24-27. His tutor was the "God of peace."

Contentment doesn't mean you necessarily like your circumstances. It means you have confidence that God is involved with you in them. It's the surrender of ourselves into His care. We have to accept the fact that God is in control, not us. We must move from "my timing, my way, my outcome" to "God's timing, God's way, God's outcome." It's all about Christ. With Christ we can learn to say, *"I can do everything, including being content, through Christ who gives me strength."* It is Christ's power that lets us to rise above our worrisome, frustrating circumstances and say, "It is well with my soul."

"A story is told of a king who was suffering from a mysterious ailment and was advised by his astrologer that he would be cured if the shirt of a contented man was brought for him to wear. People went out to all parts of the kingdom looking for such a person, and after a long search they found a man who was really happy and content. But he did not have a shirt."

Chuckle: *"So, if your house is a mess and there's no one there to see it, is it still messy?"*

Quote: *"Contentment is natural wealth, luxury is artificial poverty."* ~ Socrates

Choose to Be Content

"But godliness with contentment is great gain. For we brought nothing into the world, and we can take nothing out of it. But if we have food and clothing, we will be content with that" (1 Timothy 6:6-8 NIV).

In Philippians 4:11, Paul tells us that, over time, he had learned to be content. Have we? Or do we show evidence of our discontent? Some believe that changing their circumstances or the acquisition of material things will bring them contentment. But trying to obtain contentment from possessions is like trying to carry water in a sieve—it just "doesn't hold water."

Potential reactions to life's difficult circumstances include bitterness, depression, selfishness, and finally, contentment. Which reaction is most prevalent in your life?

Contentment comes from trusting God's sufficiency, rather than our own. The scripture speaks of many things which rob us of contentment and tells us what our response should be. *"...be content with your pay"* (Luke 3:14 NIV); *"But if we have food and clothing, we will be content with that"* (1 Timothy 6:8 NIV); *"Be content with such things as you have..."* (Hebrews 13:5 NIV). Without Christ—the inward source of contentment—you will never find it in people, places, or things. God was Paul's source of contentment everywhere and in all things. How was this possible?

He accepted and was content in all circumstances. *"... whether well fed or hungry, whether living in plenty or in want"* (Philippians 4:12 NIV). I read somewhere that we should never pull tomorrow's clouds over today's sunshine. Never cross a bridge until you come to it. Always take life one day at a time. Today is all you have. We must get over our past failures, those who have failed us, and unpleasant circumstances. Receive God's forgiveness and joyfully share His love with others.

Paul knew God would provide him strength to do all God wanted him to do. *"I can do everything through him who gives me strength"* (Philippians 4:13 NIV). Literally, Paul says, "I can do all things God asks me to do with the help of Christ who gives me the strength." This attitude is based on the foundation of our Christian faith—the all-sufficient Christ.

Paul was satisfied with his provisions. *"I am amply supplied"* (Philippians 4:18 NIV), and this is assured by the fact that *"My God will meet all your needs according to His glorious riches in Christ Jesus"* (Philippians 4:19 NIV). He did not require more than God had given him to be content.

How content are you? Are you at peace with yourself, with others, and with your Lord?

Aug 27

Chuckle: *"When you are dissatisfied and would like to go back to youth, think of Algebra."* ~ Will Rogers

Quote: *"The best of blessings, a contented mind."* ~ Horace, E*pistles*

Contentment and Circumstances

"I know how to live on almost nothing or with everything. I have learned the secret of living (being content) in every situation, whether it is with a full stomach or empty, with plenty or little. . . . And this same God who takes care of me will supply all your needs from his glorious riches, which have been given to us in Christ Jesus" (Philippians 4:12,19 NLT).

It is our natural tendency to depend on life's circumstances to determine our degree of happiness and contentment. Therefore, we focus our efforts on trying to control our circumstances. It's sometimes difficult for us to understand that the true contentment God wants for us wells up from within us and does not result from life's circumstances.

The secret to real contentment is learning to see the world from God's point of view. We learn to do this when we begin to focus our attention and effort on doing what God wants us to do rather than on what we would like to have—doing versus having. Paul did not waste his time in pursuit of wealth and possessions, but focused his energy on doing what God called him to do. He had his priorities in order when it came to his relationship with his Lord.

If we depend upon what we have to bring us contentment, we will have missed out on experiencing the kind of contentment we see in Paul. True, when we are blessed with plenty, we may experience feelings of self-satisfaction from what we have earned by our skills and perseverance. But such selfish feelings can't compare with the serenity and contentment God wants to give us by His presence within us and by our trusting His promises.

Paul was grateful for everything God had given him, whether little or much. Like Paul, we should detach ourselves from the least important and nonessential, and focus on the eternal. In God's grand scheme of things, it doesn't matter how much of this world's "stuff" we accumulate. What matters are the treasures we have laid up in heaven (see Matthew 6:19-21).

In summary, our yearning for physical comforts and possessions is our effort to fill an empty place in our hearts that only God can fill. God wants us to trust Him and rejoice in His presence rather than depending upon our circumstances to bring us contentment. Believing His promises to meet our needs brings indescribable contentment and peace.

"A Puritan sat down to his meal and found that he had only a little bread and some water. His response was to exclaim, 'What? All this and Jesus Christ, too!' Contentment is found when we have the correct perspective on life."

Aug 28

Chuckle: *A little boy had a part in the school play that read, "It is I, be not afraid." He came out on stage and said, "It's me and I'm scared!*

Quote: *"The wise man in the storm prays to God, not for safety from danger, but for deliverance from fear."* ~ Ralph Waldo Emerson

Conquering Our Fears

Then he, Jesus, asked them, "Why are you so afraid? Do you still not have faith in me?" (Mark 4:40 NLT).

Our fears have a major impact on the way we think and act. We may be keenly aware of some of our most dreaded fears, but others may be buried so deeply in our psyche that we may not even be aware of them. You may react to a situation instinctively, not fully understanding why you reacted in such a way. A deeply rooted fear may be the culprit. Fears of any intensity will ultimately control your life if you don't have the strength or courage to bring them to the surface and place them at the feet of Jesus. God wants to help us root out our fears and free us from their debilitating effects on our conduct and happiness.

Life's storms come in many forms and intensities. Think of situations that cause you the greatest anxiety. Now think about all the miracles God has performed in your life—the most important of which is your salvation by faith in Jesus Christ. If God can save your eternal soul, what makes you think He is incapable of taking away your fears? Just bare your fears and view them in light of God's past faithfulness, and they will lose their control over you.

Now back to our passage. Jesus equated the disciples' being afraid to a lack of faith in Him. The disciples feared for their lives. They were afraid the fierce storm would swamp their boat and they would drown. They were afraid even with Jesus asleep in the boat with them, and this seemed to surprise and disappoint Jesus.

I believe it disappoints our Lord when we let our fears rule our lives rather than trusting in Him in all situations.

In situations that cause you to be afraid, you have two options. You can panic, like the disciples, and assume that Jesus is no longer in control and does not care what happens to you. Or you can conquer your fears by placing your complete trust in Him as Savior and Lord in all situations.

Pastor Ray Stedman spoke to a young man who had given his heart to Christ in a Billy Graham crusade. He told him that his new life in Christ would free him from all fear of death. The young man replied, "I have never been much afraid of death. But I'll tell you what I am afraid of—I'm afraid I'll waste my life." Stedman then commented, " I believe that fear is deep within each of us. It has been put there by our Creator. No one wishes to waste his life."
~ Ray Stedman, *Authentic Christianity*

Unconquered fears can certainly result in a wasted life. But God can change all that if we only turn our lives and fears over to Him.

Aug 29

Chuckle: *We all admire different qualities in people. My grandfather used to say, "If we all liked the same thing, everybody would be after your grandmother!"*

Quote: *"Twenty years from now you will be more disappointed by the things that you didn't do than by the ones you did."*
~ Mark Twain

First Things First

"He who did not spare His own Son, but gave Him up for us all —how will He not also, along with Him, graciously give us all things?" (Romans 8:32 NIV).

Have you thought lately about what is most important in your life? Do your priorities center around pleasing God or impressing others? Are you more concerned with self-indulgence than self-sacrifice? If these questions stirred a sense of conviction in your heart, perhaps it's time to reassess your priorities and get first things first in your life. Did these questions create a desire within you to let God change you from the inside out?

If you truly wish to change things in your life, a transformation of the heart is required. Only God is able to permanently make a change take root in your life. When we rely on our own power to make changes in our lives, these adjustments generally stem from wrong motives and are temporary in nature. They may resemble new years' resolutions made in our own strength. We have good intentions when we make them, but the flesh is just too weak—the will just isn't there. We go for the quick and easy way, which usually is self-focused and not God's way.

However, His Holy Spirit within empowers us to make adjustments and transformations with eternal value. Ask Him to *"create in you a clean heart and renew a right spirit within you"* (Psalm 51:10 NIV).

If your heart is consistent with God's will, you never have to doubt His willingness to move in your life. Make a choice to build on a firm, permanent foundation. Rely fully on God alone for He loves you and will help you on your journey! Read in His Word all that He has planned for you—it's all good! He will help you keep first things first. *"I can do all everything through Him (Christ) who gives me strength"* (Philippians 4:13 NIV).

Isaac Newton's First Law of Motion states, *"Everything continues in a state of rest unless it is compelled to change by forces impressed upon it."* When you stop letting God change you, you stop growing and maturing spiritually. A change in behavior begins with a change in the heart.

Jesus asked the man by the pool of Bethesda, *"Do you want to be made well?"* Some people don't want change in their lives. They feel comfortable right where they are. Jesus was asking this man, "Are you content with the way you are right now? Do you really want your life to change?"

Aug 30

Chuckle*: What do you call a dinosaur with an extensive vocabulary? The saurus.*

Quote: *"The fruit of wisdom is Christlikeness, peace, humility, and love; and the root of it is faith in Christ as the manifested wisdom of God."* ~ J. I. Packer

Foolishness

"The man without the Spirit does not accept the things that come from the Spirit of God, for they are foolishness to him, and he cannot understand them, because they are spiritually discerned. The spiritual man makes judgments about all things, but he himself is not subject to any man's judgment: 'For who has known the mind of the Lord that he may instruct him?' But we have the mind of Christ" (1 Corinthians 2:14-16 NIV).

In this passage, Paul makes one thing abundantly clear—the person who has the Holy Spirit resident within him can understand the world from God's perspective—that is, if he relies upon the Holy Spirit in his discernments.

As Christians, we have access to the very mind of Christ through His indwelling Spirit and God's written Word. So the question is not whether God has given us the ability to discern right from wrong or good from evil, but whether or not we listen to the Holy Spirit.

In Psalm 15, the psalmist asks the question: *"Lord, who may dwell in your sanctuary? Who may live on your holy hill?"* To state the question another way: "Who will you welcome into your presence to worship you?" In the Psalm, several characteristics are listed for the person God welcomes into His presence. Verse five says, *"He who despises a vile man but honors those who fear the Lord."* This requirement is one of perspective. This person must first be able to discern what is to be despised and what is to be honored—what is good and holy in God's sight and what is vile in His sight. Such a man has a clear vision of what is good and what is evil, because he sees the world as God sees it.

As Christians, our spiritual discernment senses can become dulled so that we no longer are offended by ungodly conduct. We can find ourselves compromising our convictions and adopting some of the same moral values that God detests. I venture to say that many of us are not offended by some television programs that would have caused us to turn the TV off in disgust twenty years ago. Not only are we not offended by them, but we may have come to enjoy them. Our moral senses are no longer as keen and discerning as God wants them to be in recognizing right and wrong.

God only invites holy people into His presence for worship that pleases Him. Perhaps each of us should re-evaluate our tolerance of evil, ask God's forgiveness if we have compromised our spiritual integrity, and commit ourselves anew to holy living. Then God will invite us into His holy presence for worship.

As we seek to live holy lives, God will continue to sharpen our spiritual sensitivity with new abilities to discern between things of the Spirit and things of the world.

Aug 31

Chuckle: *Whose bright idea was it to put an "s" in the word 'lisp?*

Quote: *"The people of the world focus on what they are overcoming. Christians focus on what they are becoming."*
~ Henry Blackaby

Focus on the Future

"No, dear brothers and sisters, I am still not all I should be, but I am focusing all my energies on this one thing: Forgetting the past and looking forward to what lies ahead" (Philippians 3:13 NLT).

Today a prevalent thought is that the dominating influence in our lives is what happened in our past. If you grew up in an abusive home devoid of love and wholesome influences, those experiences will determine the course of your life.

There is no doubt that devastating experiences in our past can create severe emotional problems which must be dealt with, sometimes requiring professional help. However, it seems the world is preoccupied with the past—perhaps because the world faces such an uncertain future. As Christians, we should focus on the glorious future God has promised to us.

Paul had every reason to want to forget his past. He was a chief persecutor of the early Christians and had even held the coats of those who stoned Stephen, the first Christian martyr. We all have things in our past which we would rather forget, and we live in a state of tension between what we have been and what we want to be. But, as Christians, we must realize that Christ has overcome our past and has given us the freedom to become the persons He wants us to be.

"What this means is that those who become Christians become new persons. They are not the same anymore, for the old life is gone. A new life has begun!" (2 Corinthians 5:17 NLT). God has forgiven your sins of the past and chooses not to remember them anymore.

Because of this truth, we should not forget our past, but we should never let our past be a controlling force in our lives. Things are new and different now.

Instead of dwelling on the past, press on toward the future by growing in your knowledge of God by concentrating on your relationship with Jesus Christ right now. Realize that you have been forgiven, and then press on to a life of faith and obedience. Focus on the future and a more meaningful and fulfilling life because of your hope in Jesus Christ. Like Paul, our desire to be more like Christ should cause us to use all our energies toward that end.

If you can't shake your preoccupation with your past, ask our Heavenly Father to reveal anew the beautiful and amazing future that awaits you, and in faith, keep pressing on toward that reality.

About the Author:

Jerry Stratton grew up as the son of a Baptist minister in the beautiful mountains of Northwest Arkansas. He is a graduate of Ouachita Baptist University, Arkadelphia, Arkansas; and Baylor University, Waco, Texas. He served in the U.S. Army for a total of 30 years and retired in December, 1984.

Upon retirement from the army, Jerry sensed God's call to vocational ministry. In his 28 years of ministry, he has served as minister of education and administration, director of missions, pastor, and interim pastor. For the past eight years, he has published a daily devotional via e-mail and his personal blog. In addition to his internet devotional ministry, Jerry continues to minister through his local church and substitute preaching.

Jerry and his wife, Dotse, met at Ouachita Baptist University. They celebrated 61 years of marriage in August, 2015 and make their home in Copperas Cove, Texas. Their two wonderful children have blessed them with six fantastic grandchildren.

Made in the USA
Coppell, TX
23 January 2021

48568207R00152